*DOCUMENTS OF MODERN HISTORY*

*General Editors:*

# A. G. Dickens
The Director, Institute of Historical Research, University of London

# Alun Davies
Professor of Modern History, University College, Swansea

*FOR JANET*

# THE RENAISSANCE
# SENSE OF THE PAST

by

### Peter Burke
Lecturer in the School of European Studies, University of Sussex

Edward Arnold

First published 1969 by
Edward Arnold (Publishers) Ltd,
41 Maddox Street, London W1

Cloth edition SBN: 7131 5474 8
Paper edition SBN: 7131 5475 6

Printed in Great Britain by
Robert Cunningham and Sons Ltd, Alva

# CONTENTS

# PREFACE

This essay is not a general study of the writing of history in Western Europe between 1350 and 1650, the period with which it is concerned. All I aim to do is to disentangle some two or three strands – perhaps the most important ones – in the historical thought of that time. Similarly, the first chapter, on the Middle Ages, should not be regarded as a general assessment of medieval historians. Its function is chiefly a negative one; to help define by contrast what I believe to be the key characteristics of Renaissance historical thought. I do believe that medieval historians were as I have described them, but also that, from another point of view, these are not the most important things to say about them. Medieval historians were not aiming at being Renaissance historians – and missing; they were aiming at something else. The same point applies to the chapter on classical historical thought and the section on China. They are there to illuminate the Renaissance by comparison and contrast.

I should like to thank Professor Hugh Trevor-Roper for his encouragement of a postgraduate interest in historiography; Professor A. G. Dickens and Dr Hugh Kearney for reading the typescript, and suggesting various improvements; the 'Humans', who discussed an early draft of chapter two; Chris Stray, who read chapter six; and Professors Leopold Ettlinger, Felix Gilbert, Joseph Levine, Fritz Levy, and John Pocock, for helping me on specific points.

## *Acknowledgments*

Our thanks are due to the following for the use of copyright material: Basil Blackwell (pp. 5-6); The Bodley Head (pp. 132-3, 135); Cambridge University Press (pp. 68-9); University of Chicago Press (pp. 21-3); Columbia University Press (pp. 14-16, 84-5, 86-7); Harvard University Press and Heinemann (pp. 131-2); G. Laterza and Figli, S.P.A. (pp. 28, 125-6); The New English Library (pp. 81-2); Martinus Nijhoff, N.V. (p. 70); Penguin Books Ltd. (pp. 8-9, 42-3, 77-80, 110-11, 132-3, 135, 137-8, 140-1); G. C. Sansoni (pp. 119-20); Simon and Schuster Inc. (pp. 90-1, 108-9, 111-17), and Yale University Press (pp. 12, 55-8).

Where the source of translation has not been acknowledged it is by Peter Burke.

# I

# MEDIEVAL HISTORICAL THOUGHT

## I

This essay is concerned with the 'sense of history'. The sense of history is a complex concept: I shall define it to include three factors, each of which may be found without the others. The first factor might be called the sense of anachronism; the second, the awareness of evidence; the third, the interest in causation. This sense of history is very much a part of our culture, by which I mean that of the West since about 1800. But I wish to argue that it began to develop during the Renaissance (the fifteenth century in Italy, the sixteenth and early seventeenth centuries elsewhere), and that it was lacking in the Middle Ages. That is, surprising as this may now seem and despite (or because of) the great medieval achievements in other fields, during the whole millennium 400-1400, there was no 'sense of history' even among the educated; in fact each of the three elements was generally lacking, not just their combination. These are large claims, and before considering the Renaissance, they need to be substantiated.

First, the sense of anachronism, or sense of historical perspective, or sense of change, or sense of the past. Medieval men lacked a sense of the past being different in quality from the present. They did not deny that in some ways the past was unlike the present; they knew, for example, that the ancients had not been Christians. But they did not take the difference very seriously.

A dramatic example of this lack of perspective can be found in the *Florentine History* of the thirteenth-century chronicler Ricordano Malespini. He describes the career of Catiline, who married a woman called Belisea after he had killed her husband. Her daughter was taken away by a centurion. One day, 'when queen Belisea was at Mass in the church of Fiesole on Easter morning', the centurion went up and spoke to her. Malespini may or may not have thought that Catiline was a king; he probably did not think about the question of whether other societies had forms of political organisation different from his own. But he does know that Catiline came before Christ; twenty pages further on, he made reference to Lucca being called Lucca 'at the time that Christ was born of the Virgin Mary'. Yet he makes the 'queen' go to 'Mass'. That is an unusually explicit example of what it is like not to have a sense of the past.

Implicit examples can be multiplied. In a fifteenth-century Wakefield pageant, Herod swears 'by Mahoun in heaven': Mohammed is not thought of as a historical figure, still less one who lived after Herod. In a fifteenth-century Coventry play, there is a reference to Alexander the Great, 'that for chivalry beareth the ball'. Again, there is no idea that the institution of knighthood and the values of chivalry are not ancient. Chrétien de Troyes in the twelfth century, Lydgate in the fifteenth, declare that 'knighthood' began in Greece, then passed to Rome. The fourteenth-century cult of the Nine Worthies assimilates heroes from three cultures in a similar way. Hector, Caesar, Alexander; Joshua, David, Judas Maccabeus; Arthur, Charlemagne and Godfrey of Bouillon. Again, the German emperor was thought of as filling the same role as Augustus. Aristotle was seen as a schoolman, a 'clerk'. The best evidence of this way of thinking is not verbal but pictorial, because pictures cannot blur distinctions but have to be explicit; Alexander the Great or Moses were represented in medieval art as knights, in the armour of the day.

Three important examples of the medieval attitude to the past, which illustrate the historical innocence of their approach, their lack of historical curiosity, are their attitudes to ruins; to the Bible; and to law.

Take the case of the ruins of Rome, for example. They were there in the twelfth century; they were noticed. They were thought of as 'marvels', *mirabilia*. But they were taken as given. People seem not to have wondered how they got there, when they were built, or why the style of architecture was different from their own. The most they will do is to tell 'just so stories' or explanatory myths about the names of places.

The *Marvels of the City of Rome* (Mirabilia urbis Romae) is an anonymous work of *c.* 1150. I have taken one descriptive extract and one explanatory one.

> The theatres be these: the theatre of Titus and Vespasian at the Catacombs; the theatre of Tarquin and the Emperors at the Seven Floors; Pompey's theatre at St. Lawrence; Antoninus his theatre by

Antoninus his bridge; Alexander's theatre nigh unto Round St. Mary's; Nero's theatre nigh to Crescentius his castle; and the Flaminian theatre.

There is an arch at St. Mark's that is called Hand of Flesh, for at the time when in this city of Rome Lucy, an holy matron, was tormented for the faith of Christ by the emperor Diocletian, he commanded that she should be laid down and beaten to death; and behold, he that smote her was made stone, but his hand remained flesh, unto the seventh day; wherefore the name of the place is called Hand of Flesh to this day.

> *Marvels of Rome*, trans. F. M. Nichols, (1889)
> London and Rome, pp. 23-4, 12-13

Second, the medieval attitude to the Bible. Like the ruins of Rome, it was taken as given. Since it was the work of God, who was eternal, there was no point in asking when the different parts of it were written down. It was treated not as a historical document but as an oracle; that is, what it had meant was subordinated to what it could mean. From the time of the Fathers of the Church, the Bible was interpreted in four senses; the literal or historical sense, and three spiritual senses, allegorical, moral and anagogical.

Thomas Aquinas (1225-74) summarises the orthodox view of the interpretation of scripture in his *Summa*.

The author of Holy Writ is God, in whose power it is to signify His meaning, not by words only (as man also can do) but also by things themselves. So whereas in every other science things are signified by words, this science has the property that the things signified by the words have themselves also a signification. Therefore that first signification whereby words signify things belongs to the first sense, the historical or literal. That signification whereby things signified by words have themselves also a signification is called the spiritual sense, which is based on the literal, and presupposes it. Now this spiritual sense has a threefold division . . . so far as the things of the Old Law signify the things of the New Law, there is the allegorical sense; so far as the things done in Christ, or so far as the things which signify Christ, are types of what we ought to do, there is the moral sense. But so far as they signify what relates to eternal glory there is the anagogical sense

> St. Thomas Aquinas, *Summa Theologica*, trans.
> by Dominican Friars, (n.d., recent) London,
> question 1, 10th article, reply to objection 3

The allegorical interpretation of the Bible is of a special kind. It is 'figural'. The German literary historian Erich Auerbach defined *figura*, in his famous essay on the subject, as 'something real and historical which announces something else that is also real and historical'. The Old Testament is in general (as Aquinas noted) a figure of the New; Adam is a figure of Christ; Jonah's emergence from the whale a figure of Christ's Resurrection. It is not that Adam is simply like Christ, that he may be compared by us to Christ. In an objective sense he announces Christ. It is as if God is writing the history we live, and Adam is one of his metaphors. This kind of interpretation clearly worked against the sense of the past, for it depends on taking men and events out of their historical context, and putting them into a spiritual one.

Third, the medieval attitude to law. Laws, like the ruins of Rome and the Bible, tended to be taken as given, eternally there, discovered, not invented at a particular moment in time. New laws were – in theory – impossible; a contradiction in terms, for law was custom and custom was old by definition. King Offa of Mercia, making a grant of land shortly after the year 700, declared that 'the decrees of royal ordinances remain in unshaken stability for ever.' An example among many of the appeal to custom is that of a plea by the abbey of Holy Trinity Fécamp, about 1086, against William of Briouze.

> As to the toll which he took at his bridge from the men of Holy Trinity, it was adjudged that it ought not to be paid, because it was never paid in the time of King Edward.

Men sometimes noticed that laws differed; this led them to the conclusion that some laws were better than others, but not that laws were created in particular circumstances. King Alfred considered the possibility of applying the law of Exodus to his own kingdom. His own laws show him as prepared to abolish some of the old, but reluctant to make new laws.

> After it came about that many people had received the faith of Christ, many synods were assembled throughout the earth, and likewise throughout England, after they had received the faith of Christ, of holy bishops and also of other distinguished wise men ... they then in many synods fixed the compensation for many human misdeeds, and they wrote them in many synod-books, here one law, there another. Then I, King Alfred, collected these together and ordered to be written many of them which our forefathers observed, those which I liked; and many of them which I did not like, I rejected with the advice of my councillors, and

ordered them to be differently observed. For I dared not presume
to set in writing at all many of my own, because it was unknown
to me what would please those who should come after us.

> Laws of King Alfred, introduction, *English
> Historical Documents*, volume I (trans), ed. D.
> Whitelock, (1955) London, pp. 372-3

In the Middle Ages, the laws of Justinian were known; in the twelfth
and thirteen centuries they were studied and interpreted by the
'glossators'. These lawyers were interested in precedents; but in precedents torn from their historical context. In this sense they thought of
law as something outside time. In the mid-thirteenth century, St.
Thomas Aquinas, more aware of change than his predecessors, could
discuss the justification of altering laws, and could see that circumstances alter too; but he stresses the dangers of legal change.

As we have said above, human law is a certain dictate of reason
by which human actions are regulated. From this point of view
there can be two causes which justify a changing of human law.
The first is on the part of reason: the second on the part of men
whose actions are regulated by the law. On the part of reason,
because it would seem natural for human reason to proceed by
stages from the imperfect to the more perfect. So we see in
speculative science that those who first began to philosophise
arrived at an incomplete system which their successors later ela-
borated into something more perfect. It is the same also in practical affairs. For those who first set themselves to consider what was
useful to the common well-being of man, not being able to solve
the entire problem themselves, established certain regulations
which were imperfect and deficient in many respects; and these
regulations were later modified by their successors to retain those
which were the least defective from the point of view of the public
interest.

On the part of men, whose actions are regulated by law, changes
in law may be justified on account of altered circumstances: for
according to the different circumstances in which men are found
(*secundum diversas eorum conditiones*) different standards obtain. . . .

As has been said, change in human law is justified only to the
extent that it benefits the general welfare. Now the very fact of
change in the law is, in a certain sense, detrimental to the public
welfare. This is because, in the observance of law, custom is of
great importance: so much so, that any action which is opposed to

general custom, even if itself of little importance, always seems more serious. So when law is changed its coercive power is diminished, to the extent that custom is set aside. Thus human law should never be changed unless the benefits which result to the public interest are such as to compensate for the harm done. This may be the case if the new statutes contain great and manifest advantages; or if there is urgent necessity due to the fact that the old law contains evident injustice, or its observance is excessively harmful. So the Jurisconsult says that 'in passing new constitutions their utility must be very evident before renouncing those laws which have long been regarded as equitable' [Ulpian, *Digest*, i.IV.2].

> St. Thomas Aquinas, *Summa Theologica*, trans. in A. P. D'Entrèves, ed., *Aquinas: Selected Political Writings*, (1959) Oxford, question 1, 10th article

To sum up. Medieval men lacked a sense of the 'differentness' of the past. They saw it in terms of the present; they projected themselves back on to the men of the past. Sometimes this proved impossible: the past was too obviously different. In these cases, one of two things happened. One possibility was for them to see the men of the past as strange foreigners. The thirteenth-century architect Villard de Honnecourt called a Roman tomb, which he could not see as contemporary, 'the tomb of a Saracen'. One might say that the sense of space was being used as a substitute for the sense of time. As Racine observed in his second preface to *Bajazet* (defending his choice of a subject which was not classical but Turkish):

> . . . geographical distance in some sense makes up for too great a proximity in time: for the people scarcely distinguishes between what is, if I may so put it, a thousand years away and that which is a thousand leagues away from them.

A second possibility was to see the men of the past as not quite human, whether gods or devils. This was not such a different strategy (an unconscious strategy, I should emphasise), since foreigners too were often regarded as not quite human. So, for example, Vergil, whose epic was so different from medieval epic, was seen as a necromancer. Again, an Anglo-Saxon poem, 'The Ruin', identifies a Roman city, often identified as Bath, as the work of giants.

> Wondrous is this wall-stone; broken by fate, the castles have decayed; the work of giants is crumbling.

**2**

The second element in the sense of history as I have defined it is awareness of evidence. Medieval writers and scholars compared to those of
the Renaissance took an uncritical attitude towards evidence. This
attitude has two aspects, which one might label 'active' and 'passive'.

The passive aspect is the acceptance of 'authority'. Men acted as if
they believed that because something was written, it must be true; every
'author' was an 'authority' and what he wrote was 'authentic'. (The
related words remind us that the ideas were once related too.) The rela-
tive reliability of sources is rarely distinguished; the most one is likely
to find is a medieval historian like Bede distinguishing what he has had
from an eyewitness from other kinds of information; and such distinctions are not commonly made. Historical narratives tended to
resemble 'bricolage', compositions from ready-made fragments, for
the historian would often incorporate the actual words of the 'authority',
making a mosaic of the different authors. There was, anyway, no
objection to plagiarism, in history as in literature. The existence of this
method is not so surprising: scissors-and-paste history still exists, after
all – what is surprising is only its dominance. Gregory of Tours, re-
counting a miracle, mentions that he was present at the time but 'not
worthy to see it' (*haec videre non merui*). In other words, he puts testimony before the evidence of his senses. Bede lived near Hadrian's Wall,
but when he had occasion to describe it, he preferred to incorporate a
ready-made description by Vegetius into his text. Even Dante thinks
of Livy – Livy of all people – as 'Livy who never makes a mistake'
(*Livio che non erra*).

The 'active' side of this attitude to evidence is the frame of mind
which makes it possible to invent myths and retail them as history, and
to forge documents.

Medieval history-writing is full of myths, secular and religious. (I
define myth as fiction passing as fact). In the thirteenth century, for
example, the Florentines believed that Florence had been founded by
Caesar: the British believed that Britain had been colonised by Brutus
the Trojan; the French believed that they had been converted by
Dionysius the Areopagite, the Athenian baptised by St. Paul, and
that he was their 'St Denis': the Spaniards believed that St. James had
appeared in the ninth century to help them defeat the Moors. Saint's
lives, favourite medieval reading- and listening-matter, were especially
full of what has been called 'hagiographic myth'. It is difficult to be

sure how the myths arose. There is myth-as-explanation: some of them seem to have started as attempts to explain an obscure name or picture of a saint or secular hero. There is myth-as-mixture: conflations of stories about different people. The Spanish story of St. James, the twin brother of Christ, appearing on a white horse to defeat the Moors, seems to have something to do with the older story of the twins Castor and Pollux, on white horses, winning a battle in Italy in 449 BC. The story of the conversion of France seems to derive from a confusion between a Dionysius and a Denys. Confusion is all the easier because of the lack of a sense of historical perspective, so that all events take place in 'mythical time'. More important still is myth-as-justification: a story about the past which justifies, and was presumably invented to justify, a present situation (see p. 18 below for a fuller discussion of this). St. James was both an encouragement to resist the Moors and a justification of the payments made by Spaniards to the canons of the cathedral of St. James at Compostela. King Arthur, who was put into general circulation by Geoffrey of Monmouth in the twelfth century, was an encouragement to British national pride, and a justification of the claims of the Norman dynasty to be on a level with the Capetians, who saw themselves as heirs of the hero Charlemagne. Two English kings quoted Geoffrey in support of their claims to dominion over Scotland.

In the case of myths, one can never be sure of tracking down the original teller. It is always possible that the man we believe invented a story, did no more than pass it on – or perhaps the story grew by half-conscious additions, as by borrowings from stories about other people, and was not 'invented' at all. There is this uncertainty in the case of Geoffrey of Monmouth's account of Trojan migration to Britain.

Geoffrey of Monmouth (d. *c.* 1155) was a cleric and the probable author of the *History of the Kings of Britain*, which put the celebrated Brutus legend into general currency. Brutus is described as the son of Silvius, who was the son of Ascanius, who was the son of Aeneas. I have included two extracts, the prophecy of the goddess Diana (compare *Aeneid* VI) and the landing in Britain.

> It seems to him that the goddess stood before him and spoke these words to him: 'Brutus, beyond the setting of the sun, past the realms of Gaul, there lies an island in the sea, once occupied by giants. Now it is empty and ready for your folk. Down the years this will prove an abode suited to you and your people: and for your descendants it will be a second Troy. A race of kings will be born

there from your stock and the round circle of the whole earth will be subject to them.'

When he awoke from this vision, the leader remained in doubt as to whether it had been a dream which he had experienced or whether the living goddess really had prophesied the land to which he should travel. In the end he called his comrades together and told them in full detail what had happened to him in his sleep. They were delighted and advised him to turn back to the ships and to travel westwards under full sail in search of what the goddess had promised them, while the wind still blew fair. . . .

[Brutus and his men landed at Totnes in Cornwall.] At this time the island of Britain was called Albion. It was uninhabited except for a few giants. It was, however, most attractive, because of the delightful situation of its various regions, its forests and the great number of its rivers, which teemed with fish; and it filled Brutus and his comrades with a great desire to live there. When they had explored the different districts, they drove the giants they had discovered into the caves in the mountains. With the approval of their leader they divided the land among themselves. They began to cultivate the fields and to build houses, so that in a short time you would have thought that the land had always been inhabited. Brutus then called the island Britain from his own name. . . .

> Geoffrey of Monmouth, *History of the Kings of Britain*, trans. L. Thorpe, (1966) London, pp. 65, 72

Some famous examples of 'hagiographic myth' may be found in the *Golden Legend* of Jacopo da Varazze (Jacobus de Voragine) *c.* 1228-98, a Dominican friar who became archbishop of Genoa. For example, his life of St. Jerome tells the story of the lion who limped into Jerome's monastery with a wounded foot, was cured by him, and became quite tame thereafter – the lion who so often appears in pictures of St. Jerome. Again, he tells the story of Dionysius, or Denys: his conversion by Paul and his visit to France.

> Denis the Areopagite was converted to Christianity by St. Paul. He was called 'Areopagite' from the quarter of the town in which he lived. The Areopagus was the quarter of Mars, because there was a temple dedicated to that god there. The Athenians gave each part of the town the name of the god who was worshipped there; thus this quarter was called 'Areopagus' because Ares is one of the names of Mars: the quarter where Pan was wor-

shipped was called the Panophagus, and so on. The Areopagus was the most famous quarter, because it was that of the nobility and the schools of liberal arts. That was why Denis lived there, a very great philosopher who was called Theosophus, friend of God, because of his learning and his perfect knowledge of the divine names . . . when St. Paul came to Athens, the stoic and epicurean philosophers disputed with him. Some said, 'what does this wind-bag want to say?' Others: 'he seems to be teaching new gods.' So they took him to the quarter of the philosophers to examine this new doctrine there, and they said to him: 'you have told us certain things which we have never heard before; we want very much to know about them.' The Athenians spent all their time discussing novelties. When St. Paul saw the altars of the gods as he passed, among others the altar of the unknown god, he said to these philosophers: 'the god whom you worship without know-ing him is the God I come to preach to you as the true God who created heaven and earth.' Then he said to St. Denis, whom he saw to be the best theologian, 'Denis, what is this unknown god?' Denis replied: 'He is the true God, whose existence has not yet been proved like that of the other gods; he is unknown to us, he is hidden; it is he who will come at a later time and reign for ever and ever.' Paul said to him: 'Is he man or spirit only?' 'He is god and man', replied Denis, 'he is only unknown because he lives in the heavens.' St. Paul said, 'It is he whom I preach; he descended from heaven, took flesh, was put to death and rose again on the third day.' Denis was still engaged in discussion with Paul when a blind man passed by; immediately the Areopagite said to Paul: 'if you say to that blind man in the name of your God, "see" and he sees, I will believe immediately; but do not use any magic formula, for you know well where that power comes from. I will tell you what words to use. Say to him: "in the name of Jesus Christ born of a virgin, crucified, dead, who rose again and ascen-ded into heaven, see."' To avoid all suspicion of magic, St. Paul told Denis to say the words himself. When Denis told the blind man to see, he immediately recovered his sight. So Denis and his wife Damaria and his whole family were baptised. He was in-structed by St. Paul for three years and ordained bishop of Athens, where he gave himself up to preaching and converted to Christ-ianity the city and a great part of the country.

It is said that St. Paul revealed to him what he had seen when he was caught up to the third heaven; St. Denis himself seems to suggest this in many places: and in treating of the hierarchies of angels, their choirs and their functions, he expresses himself with such wisdom and clarity that you would think that he had not learned of these things at second hand but rather that he had been caught up to the third heaven himself and that he had seen everything he describes . . . he was present at the dormition of the Virgin, as he seems to suggest in the third chapter of his book on *The Divine Names*. When he learned that St. Peter and St. Paul were imprisoned at Rome by order of Nero, he asked a bishop to take over from him and went to visit them. After they had been martyred, St. Clement, who was the head of the Church, sent him to France together with Rusticus and Eleutherus. He was sent to Paris where he converted many people to the faith, built many churches and placed in them monks of different orders.

Jacopo da Varazze, *The Golden Legend*

Besides the creation of myths, what one also finds in the Middle Ages is the production of documents which were not by their reputed authors. There are the works of 'pseudo-Dionysius', for example, the treatises on the celestial and ecclesiastical hierarchies and on the divine names probably written about the year 500 by a Syrian monk, but ascribed to Dionysius the Areopagite, as is done in the biography by Jacopo da Varazze which has just been reproduced. Then there is 'pseudo-Isidore', the collection of canons (laws of the Church) ascribed to Isidore of Seville, *c.* 560–636. This collection contains many forged papal letters. They were not invented so much as borrowed; patchworks of quotations from the Bible, the Fathers, the Laws of the Visigoths, and so on. These borrowings were made without any sense of anachronism: as a modern writer puts it, 'the pseudo-Isidore made his popes of the first and second centuries write in Frankish Latin of the ninth, discourse on doctrinal controversies in the spirit of post-Nicene orthodoxy, quote documents that had not yet been composed, and issue rulings on questions that had never yet arisen.' The reason for all this is, again, justification: the defence of the rights of the Frankish Church in general and of the bishops in particular. The most famous of medieval forgeries is the Donation of Constantine, a document in which the emperor Constantine is made to give pope Sylvester I and his successors temporal power over Italy. It was probably written in the papal chancery in the mid-eighth century. Its function is obvious; it is also interesting to see how it grew out of myth, out of stories about Sylvester, like the one, referred to in the Donation itself, about Sylvester curing Constantine of leprosy. The function of this story was presumably to provide a suitable motive for the emperor giving Italy away. And so:

> we – together with all our satraps, and the whole senate and our nobles, and also all the people subject to the government of glorious Rome – considered it advisable that as the blessed Peter is seen to have been constituted vicar of the son of God on the earth, so the pontiffs who are the representatives of that same chief of the apostles, should obtain from us and our empire the power of a supremacy greater than the clemency of our earthly imperial serenity is seen to have conceded to it . . . wherefore . . . we give over and relinquish to the aforesaid our most blessed pontiff, Sylvester, the universal pope, as well our palace, as has been said, as also the city of Rome, and all the provinces, places and cities of Italy and the western regions, and we decree by this our godlike and pragmatic sanction that they are to be controlled by him and his successors, and we grant that they shall remain under the law of the holy Roman Church. Wherefore we have perceived it to be fitting that our empire and the power of our kingdom should be transferred in the regions of the East, and that in the province of Byzantia, in the most fitting place, a city should be built in our name, and that our empire should there be established, for where the supremacy of priests and the head of the christian religion has been established by the heavenly emperor, it is not right that there an earthly emperor should have jurisdiction.
>
> *The Donation of Constantine*, trans. and ed.
> C. B. Coleman, (1922) New Haven, pp. 13-17

It would be impossible to list here all the documents which were forged during the Middle Ages; but two of the more celebrated ones deserve a passing mention. In the time of the Fathers of the Church it was believed that Seneca, like Dionysius, had been converted by St. Paul and that the two men had written to one another. In the eleventh century, Seneca's letters to Paul made their appearance. In the twelfth century, the payments to the cathedral of St. James of Compostela received documentary justification, when a diploma of Ramiro I was 'discovered', ordering the payments to be made.

For students of medieval attitudes to the past, it is important to reconstitute the state of mind of these forgers. In fact, 'forgers' were just what they were not. To be a historical 'forger', as we now understand the term, is impossible without a sense of historical perspective.

It is necessary to realise the difference between past and present, to regret it, and then to pretend that the difference is not there. It is necessary to be aware of anachronisms and to avoid them. Now in this sense the medieval forgeries are not forgeries. The Pseudo-Isidore and the Donation of Constantine were written by men without a sense of anachronism. Many details in these documents show this. But if the authors lacked a sense of change, it is likely that they really thought that Constantine must have made the pope his heir; that the law of the Church was as the forged decretals say; and so on. In the case of the diploma of Ramiro I, there was a tradition to the effect that a vow of this kind had been made by Ramiro II (again, we see the telescoping of time, the confusion between different men, characteristic of myth) after the battle of Simancas in 939. Again, the confection of the false decretals was more like the creation of a legend or myth than the perpetration of a forgery. A modern writer has compared the borrowing of passages from the Fathers to make up the decretals to the borrowing of details from the life of one saint to make up a life for another. This is not to say that some forgeries may not have been deliberate attempts to cheat; we simply lack the necessary evidence to decide exactly how much innocence and how much unscrupulousness went into the making of a document like the Donation of Constantine.

## 3

The third element in the sense of history I defined as interest in causation; and this, too, was lacking in the Middle Ages. It is not that motives and causes were never mentioned; but rather that they were not seen as problematic, as controversial, or in need of evidence. Compared to modern ones, medieval histories lacked a middle ground between the ascription of motive to individuals, often done in a somewhat stereotyped way and then incorporated into the narrative without discussion, and extremely general interpretations of history in a theological manner.

The lack of interest in explanation is connected with the formal structure of medieval histories; their framework is predominantly annalistic. The origin of medieval histories is in the margin of Easter-Tables: the margin was filled with brief notes of events which happened in a particular year. When independent histories began to be written, they kept this chronicle-framework. This framework tends to organise facts in a one-thing-after-another way; and so to exclude explanation. The favourite connective is not 'because' or 'as a result' but 'meanwhile'.

An example of narrative at its most bare is the Anglo-Saxon Chro-

nicle. It is extant in several differing versions; this version, called the
Parker Chronicle, now at Corpus Christi College, Cambridge, was
made at Winchester.

> 880 (879). In this year the host went to Cirencester from Chippen-
> ham, and remained there one year. And this year a band of pirates
> gathered and took up quarters at Fulham on Thames. And the
> same year the sun was eclipsed for one hour of the day.
>
> 901 (899). In this year died Alfred, son of Aethelwulf, six nights
> before All Hallows' Day. He was king over all England except
> that part which was under Danish domination, and he ruled the
> kingdom twenty-eight and a half years. Then Edward, his son,
> succeeded to the kingdom.
>
> > *The Anglo-Saxon Chronicle*, trans. G. N.
> > Garmondsway, (1953) London, pp. 76, 91-2

A second important genre is the universal history, the history of the
world organised around such concepts as the six ages or the four
empires, and designed to show the acts of God in history. In the fifth
century bishop Orosius wrote a famous universal history: in the twelfth
century bishop Otto of Freising wrote another – *The Two Cities*.
Otto *c.* 1111-58, was bishop of Freising in Bavaria. His book, as one
might have expected from the title, is in the Augustinian tradition. He
keeps his eyes fixed on the City of God, Jerusalem, and often misses
the significance of what is happening in the City of Man, or Babylon.

> Inasmuch as there are two cities – the one of time, the other of
> eternity; the one of the earth, earthly; the other of heaven,
> heavenly; the one of the devil, the other of Christ – ecclesiastical
> writers have declared that the former is Babylon, the other
> Jerusalem. But, whereas many of the Gentiles have written much
> regarding one of these cities, to hand down to posterity the great
> exploits of men of old (the many evidences of their merits, as they
> fancied), they have yet left to us the task of setting forth what, in
> the judgement of our writers, is rather the tale of human miseries.
> There are extant in this field the famous works of Pompeius
> Trogus, Justin, Cornelius [Tacitus], Varro, Eusebius, Jerome,
> Orosius, Jordanes, and a great many others of our number, as
> well as of their array, whom it would take too long to enumerate;
> in those writings the discerning reader will be able to find not so
> much histories as pitiful tragedies made up of mortal woes. We
> believe that this has come to pass by what is surely a wise and
> proper dispensation of the Creator, in order that, whereas men in

their folly desire to cleave to earthly and transitory things, they
may be frightened away from them by their own vicissitudes, if
by nothing else, so as to be directed by the wretchedness of this
fleeting life from the creature to a knowledge of the Creator. . . .
I have undertaken therefore to bring down as far as our own time,
according to the ability that God has given me, the record of the
conflicts and miseries of the one city, Babylon; and furthermore,
not to be silent concerning our hopes regarding that other city,
but (so far as I can gather hints from the Scriptures) to make mention also of its citizens, who are now sojourning in the worldly
city. In this work I follow most of all those illustrious lights of the
Church, Augustine and Orosius, and have planned to draw from
their fountains what is pertinent to my theme and my purpose. . .

In the one thousand one hundred and forty-third year from the
incarnation of the Lord, Kaloiohannes, the emperor of Constantinople (who had entered upon a treaty of friendship with the
Roman king Conrad through a betrothal of his own son Manuel
and the sister of Queen Gertrude), entered Syria with a very large
army because Raymond prince of Antioch had sworn to give him
that province, together with the city itself, in consideration of a
sum of money, but had not kept his promise. But the venerable
bishop of Djebele manfully resisted him to his face and fearlessly
warned him, in the names of the bishop of Rome and the emperor,
to desist from his attack upon the city I have mentioned, because it
was in the possession of Latins. But John, since he had been deceived
by the prince, though he spared the city, ravaged the entire province
with fire and sword and even drove out the hermits, of whom there
is a large number in that district, from their cells and treated them
most cruelly. Herein he did not play the part of a 'Kalo' – that is
to say, a 'Good' – John. Not long afterwards, while he was
following the hunt and was using poisoned arrows, he was unexpectedly wounded by one of them. Thus this wealthy king died
very wretchedly in the midst of his army and left the throne to his
son Manuel.

At the same time Fulk, king of Jerusalem, died and surrendered
the helm of state to his son Fulk, then a mere stripling. Manuel,
on his elevation to the throne, sent messengers to King Conrad
with precious gifts (even as his father had done before) and renewed
the treaty. . . .

During these days the cities of Italy waxed insolent on account
of the king's absence. The Venetians waged fierce warfare against

the people of Ravenna, the men of Verona and of Vicenza against
the Paduans and the inhabitants of Treviso, the Pisans and the
Florentines against the men of Lucca and Siena: they filled almost
all Italy with bloodshed, rapine and fire.

> Otto of Freising, *The Two Cities*, slightly
> adapted from C. C. Mierow's trans., (1928)
> New York, pp. 93-5, 437-8

Villani has his eyes on the ground more than Otto of Freising, but
his explanations tend to be stereotyped moral ones. Giovanni Villani
(*c.* 1280-1348) was a layman, sometime prior of the republic of Florence
and master of the mint. His chronicle runs from the origin of Florence
till 1346. It was continued by his brother Matteo and Matteo's son
Filippo.

In these times the city of Pistoia being in happy and great and
good estate, among the other citizens there was one family very
noble and puissant, not however of very ancient lineage, which
was called the Cancellieri, born of one Ser Cancelliere, which was
a merchant, and gained much wealth, and by his two wives had
many sons, which by reason of their riches all became knights,
and men of worth and substance, and from them were born many
sons and grandsons, so that at this time they numbered more than
100 men in arms, rich and puissant and of many affairs, so that not
only were they the leading citizens of Pistoia, but they were
among the most puissant families of Tuscany. There arose among
them through their exceeding prosperity, and through the suggestion of the devil, contempt and emnity, between them which
were born of one wife, against them which were born of the
other; and the one part took the name of the Black Cancellieri,
and the other of the Whites. and this grew till they fought together, but it was not any great affair. And one of those on the
side of the White Cancellieri, having been wounded, they on the
side of the Black Cancellieri, to the end they might be at peace and
concord with them, sent him which had done the injury and
handed him over to the mercy of them which had received it,
that they should make amends and vengeance for it at their will;
they on the side of the White Cancellieri, ungrateful and proud,
having neither pity nor love, cut off the hand of him which had
been commended to their mercy on a horse manger. By which sin-
ful beginning, not only was the house of the Cancellieri divided,
but many violent deaths arose therefrom, and all the city of
Pistoia was divided, for some held with one part and some with

the other, and they called themselves the Whites and the Blacks, forgetting among themselves the Guelf and the Ghibelline parties; and many civil strifes and much peril and loss of life arose therefrom in Pistoia; and not only in Pistoia, but afterwards the city of Florence and all Italy was contaminated by the said parties. . . .

> Giovanni Villani, *Florentine Chronicles*, ed.
> Philip Wicksteed and trans. Rose Selfe, (1906)
> London, book VIII, chapter 38

Froissart, again, tells a vivid story and is very much concerned with this world. But he takes motives for granted. His aim was, he said, to record great deeds of arms, to encourage his readers to do likewise. In the service of this aim he tells a story which tends to decompose into anecdotes which show knights behaving in a knightly way, to be imitated, or occasionally in a villainous way, to be avoided.

Jean Froissart, *c.* 1333-*c.* 1400, from Hainault, was a cleric but lived at courts and wrote for nobles. A famous passage from his Chronicle of France, England, and Spain in his day is that describing the battle of Crecy. Important in that description are two anecdotes, given here.

The valiant king of Bohemia was killed there. He was called Charles of Luxembourg; for he was the son of the gallant king and emperor, Henry of Luxembourg: having heard the order of the battle, he enquired where his son, the lord Charles, was: his attendants answered, that they did not know, but believed he was fighting. The king said to them: 'Gentlemen, you are all my people, my friends and brothers in arms this day: therefore, as I am blind, I request of you to lead me so far into the engagement that I may strike one stroke with my sword.' The knights replied, they would directly lead him forward; and in order that they might not lose him in the crowd, they fastened all the reins of their horses together, and put the king at their head, that he might gratify his wish, and advanced towards the enemy. The lord Charles of Bohemia, who already signed his name as king of Germany, and bore the arms, had come in good order to the engagement; but when he perceived that it was likely to turn out against the French, he departed, and I do not well know what road he took. The king his father had ridden in among the enemy, and made good use of his sword; for he and his companions had fought most gallantly. They had advanced so far that they were all killed; and the next day they were found on the ground, with their horses all tied together. . . .

Early in the day, some French, German and Savoyards had broken through the archers of the prince's battalion [Prince of Wales] and had engaged with the men at arms; upon which the second battalions came to his aid, and it was time, for otherwise he would have been hard pressed. The first division, seeing the danger they were in, sent a knight, in great haste to the king of England, who was posted upon an eminence near a windmill. On the knight's arrival he said, 'Sir, the earl of Warwick, the lord Stafford, the lord Reginald Cobham, and the others who are about your son, are vigorously attacked by the French; and they entreat that you would come to their assistance with your battalion, for if their numbers should increase, they fear he will have too much to do.' The king replied, 'Is my son dead, unhorsed, or so badly wounded that he cannot support himself?' 'Nothing of the sort, thank God' rejoined the knight; 'but he is in so hot an engagement that he has great need of your help.' The king answered, 'Now Sir Thomas, return back to those that sent you, and tell them from me, not to send again for me this day, or expect that I shall come, let what will happen, as long as my son has life; and say, that I command them to let the boy win his spurs. . . .'

J. Froissart, *Chronicles*, slightly adapted from trans. by T. Johnes, (1839) London, pp. 166-7

## 4

The medieval attitude to history is itself a historical phenomenon re-requiring explanation: it needs to be related to other aspects of medie-val thought and society. A comparison between the attitude to the past in some primitive societies and in medieval Europe may help make this point clear. Anthropologists have often pointed out that the primitive societies which they studied lack any sense of historical perspective. Franz Boas said of the Eskimo that for them, the world has always been as it now is. Claude Lévi-Strauss treats the absence of a sense of historical perspective as a distinctive feature of 'la pensée sauvage'. There are several reasons for this. One is the slow pace of social change, which makes such change as does occur more difficult to notice. A second reason is that primitive societies are societies without writing; the stories they tell are handed down by oral tradition. Now in all societies there is a temptation to use the past to justify the present; as Bronislaw Malinowski pointed out, myth (about the past) can only be understood if it is seen as the charter of (present) institutions. Societies without writing can blur the distinction between past and present by revising their accounts of the past to fit in with change, and to persuade themselves that change does not happen. A dramatic example of this revision has been given by the anthropologist Jack Goody. The state of Gonja in Northern Ghana, he says, had seven divisions in 1900, and these divisions were explained by a historical myth about the founder of the state and his seven sons, who were given a share each. By 1956, when he arrived there, the British had reduced the divisions to five; but the sons of the founder had been reduced to five as well.

To return to the Middle Ages. There was social change, but it was relatively slow. There was literacy, but it was confined to few, and those few, until the end of the period, were mainly clerics. It was thus easier for orally-transmitted myths about an unchanging past to flourish. Medieval society, ruled by custom, could not afford the awareness of the difference between past and present and the consequent irrelevance of precedent. Again, other parts of medieval culture reinforced this lack of awareness of change. The static quality of medieval views of nature has recently been pointed out. For Isidore of Seville, for example, the four seasons are distinct entities: that is, as a modern writer puts it, 'where we see change, Isidore saw successive and discontinuous states of being'. Students of physics in the twelfth and thirteenth centuries made the assumption that the state of rest was the natural condition of everything in the universe. Similarly, Hugh of St. Victor (d. 1141) thought of change in history as a decline from the stability of Paradise. It may also be relevant that much medieval history was written by the monks, and that monks were professionally concerned, one might say, with the timeless. A medieval expression for entering a monastery was 'leaving time behind' (*relinquere saeculum*). 'Secular' and 'temporal' are words which remind us of this despite the connexion between 'templum' and 'tempus' at an earlier period. Another point, emphasised by Marc Bloch, is a technological one; he suggests that until mechanical clocks were used in the mid-fourteenth century, medieval men 'lived in a world in which the passage of time escaped their grasp all the more because they were so ill-equipped to measure it'.

Lacking historical perspective, medieval men were necessarily uncritical about evidence; for historical criticism depends on seeing the 'sources' not as given but as themselves the product of historical forces, telling one more about their writer or the time in which they were written than about their hero and the time they are describing. It may well be that reverence for 'authority', for the written word, was greater because books were few and writing a rare accomplishment. As for medieval 'forgeries', perhaps they should be related to the rise of literacy. Men knew that certain customs had been observed and had not been written down. They were justified by tradition and explanatory myth. Now documents were beginning to be required, as evidence of landownership, for example. At a time of transition from oral to written evidence, the manufacture of written evidence for what had been justified orally must have seemed less heinous than forgery seems now.

The last point needing explanation is the medieval attitude to motive and cause. Medieval scientists 'moralised the universe'. That is, they considered it 'better' to be a tree than to be a stone, better to be a horse than to be a tree; better to be at rest than moving, and so on. It is the less surprising that medieval historians moralised history, explaining warfare by the Italians 'waxing insolent', or the men of Pistoia being tempted by the devil. The Dutch historian Johan Huizinga has suggested that 'the symbolic mentality was an obstacle to causal thought, as causal and genetic relations must needs look insignificant by the side of symbolic connexions'. Cause and symbol coexisted during the Renaissance: but they conflicted in the seventeenth century, and in history, as in science, it was cause which won.

It would be ironic to criticise the Middle Ages for their lack of awareness of change and development and not notice that the Middle Ages was itself a period of development. In the twelfth, thirteenth and fourteenth centuries, increasing qualifications have to be made in the picture as presented so far. In the twelfth century, William of Newburgh shows a scepticism about the stories told by Geoffrey of Monmouth which implies a critical attitude to evidence; and Guibert of Nogent's doubts about the authenticity of certain relics are written in the same spirit. The legal historian Ernst Kantorowicz has argued that in the thirteenth century there is a new conception of the nature of time which emphasises change more; the scholastic philosophers inserted a new category of time, *aevum*, between *aeternitas* and *tempus*. In the same century, the draughtsman of a law of Frederick II of Sicily had enough sense of historical perspective to write that new laws were needed as a result of *rerum mutationes et temporum*. (It is tempting, but it would be succumbing to an anachronism I am trying to label 'medieval', to translate *rerum mutationes et temporum* as 'social change'.) If the Renaissance sense of history begins with Petrarch (Francesco Petrarca, 1304-74), the new start is not unrelated to what has gone before.

# II

# THE SENSE OF THE PAST

## 1   The Antiquarian Movement

A hundred years ago, it was the custom to refer to Petrarch as the 'first
modern man'. Nowadays, such characterisations are out of favour; but
in the history of the sense of history, it is difficult not to start with him.
He reveres the ancients – as men, not as magicians; and is acutely aware
of the difference between their age and his own. He would have liked
to have lived in Augustan Rome. For him, the period before the conversion of Constantine (the *aetas antiqua*) was an age of light; the *aetas
nova*, the modern age which had succeeded it, was an age of darkness.
This was the reversal of the traditional Christian distinction; its importance was that because Petrarch rated the past above the present, he
was driven to escape from the present, to forget 'these regions, these
times, and these customs' and to relive the Roman past. Eloquent
testimony of his desire to revive and relive the past is the collection of
his letters to classical authors; this one to Livy for example.

> I should wish (if it were permitted from on high) either that I
> had been born in thine age or thou in ours; in the latter case our
> age itself, and in the former I personally, should have been the
> better for it. I should surely have been one of those pilgrims who
> visited thee. For the sake of seeing thee I should have gone not
> merely to Rome, but indeed, from either Gaul or Spain I should
> have found my way to thee as far as India. As it is, I must fain be
> content with seeing thee as reflected in thy works – not thy whole
> self, alas, but that portion of thee which has not yet perished, not-
> withstanding the sloth of our age. We know that thou didst write
> one hundred and forty-two books on Roman affairs. With what
> fervor, with what unflagging zeal must thou have laboured; and
> of that entire number there are now extant scarcely thirty.
> Oh, what a wretched custom is this of wilfully deceiving our-

selves! I have said 'thirty', because it is common for all to say so.
I find, however, that even from these few there is one lacking.
They are twenty-nine in all, constituting three decades, the first,
the third, and the fourth, the last of which has not the full number
of books. It is over these small remains that I toil whenever I wish
to forget these regions, these times, and these customs. Often I am
filled with bitter indignation against the morals of today, when
men value nothing except gold and silver, and desire nothing
except sensual, physical pleasures. If these are to be considered the
goal of mankind, then not only the dumb beasts of the field, but
even insensible and inert matter has a richer, a higher goal than
that proposed to itself by thinking man. But of this elsewhere.

It is now fitter that I should render thee thanks, for many
reasons indeed, but for this in especial: that thou didst so frequently cause me to forget the present evils, and transfer me to
happier times. As I read, I seem to be living in the midst of the
Cornellii Scipiones Africani, of Laelius, Fabius Maximus, Metellus,
Brutus and Decius, of Cato, Regulus, Cursor, Torquatus, Valerius Corvinus, Salinator, of Claudius, Marcellus, Nero, Aemilius,
of Fulvius, Flaminius, Attilius, Quintius, Curius, Fabricius, and
Camillus. It is with these men that I live at such times and not
with the thievish company of today among whom I was born
under an evil star. And oh, if it were my happy lot to possess thee
entire, from what other great names would I not seek solace for
my wretched existence, and forgetfulness of this wicked age!
Since I cannot find all these in what I now possess of thy work, I
read of them here and there in other authors, and especially in that
book where thou art to be found in thy entirety, but so briefly
epitomised that, although nothing is lacking as far as the number
of books is concerned, everything is lacking as regards the value
of the contents themselves.

Pray greet in my behalf thy predecessors Polybius and Quintus
Claudius and Valerius Antias, and all those whose glory thine own
greater light has dimmed; and of the later historians, give greeting
to Pliny the Younger, of Verona, a neighbor of thine, and also to
thy former rival Crispus Sallustius. Tell them that their ceaseless
nightly vigils have been of no more avail, have had no happier lot,
than thine.

Farewell forever, thou matchless historian!

Written in the land of the living, in that part of Italy and in that
city in which I am now living and where thou wert once born and

buried, in the vestibule of the Temple of Justina Virgo, and in view of thy very tombstone, on the twenty-second of February, in the thirteen hundred and fiftieth year from the birth of Him whom thou wouldst have seen, or of whose birth thou couldst have heard, hadst thou lived a little longer.

> F. Petrarch, 'Familiar Letters', XXIV, 8, trans.
> in M. E. Cosenza, *Petrarch's Letters to Classical*
> *Authors*, (1910) Chicago

Unlike medieval writers, Petrarch did not take the ruins of Rome for granted. He was, one might say, the first modern antiquarian, in the sense of someone who is interested in the reconstruction of the past from its physical remains. He explored the Roman ruins with fra Giovanni Colonna. In his epic poem about Scipio, *Africa*, he made an attempt at the imaginative reconstruction of the Rome of Scipio's time, in the form of the description of a guided tour given to the Carthaginian envoys. Hence Miss Beryl Smalley has called the *Africa* 'an attempt at an historical novel'. Here is an excerpt from his descrip- of the Carthaginians' visit.

The visitors first passed the marble threshold of the Appian gate. Soon they saw the Walls of Pallas, forming a great circle on the hill where Evander's palace was built, the first building of note in the new town.... On their right was Mount Coelius, on their left Mount Aventinus ... then they admired the temple of the Sun and the golden temple of the Earth; they climbed, trembling, the Capitol Hill and thought that they touched the sky itself.... There they saw the Temple of Jupiter, the most splendid of all, the riches placed at the top of the hill, the thresholds thick with countless spoils, snow-white chariots and arms taken from the enemy, the golden crowns of great kings, sceptres and bracelets, necklaces torn from the necks which had worn them; ivory saddles and jewelled bridles, all arranged in order. Here they recognised their own shields, fragments of their ships, Cartha- ginian standards and breastplates. These relics of ancient wars filled them all with silent grief. As they passed through the temple they noticed, briefly, the silver bird whose voice warned of the attack of the Gauls. They went on, seeing strong men and stately women, great houses and arches loaded with the different spoils of war, triumphal standards, battles carved in the solid marble, and rich tombs. They were shown aquaducts, both above ground and below. Then in the valley of Subura they saw the palace of

Caesar, the holder of supreme power. Then they left the valley, and wearily climbed the Esquiliae and the Viminal Hill, crossed the Quirinal Hill and saw two naked giants, the work of Praxiteles and Phidias, equal in the contest for fame. There they trembled to see the palaces of the Scipios, high, with great walls and strong towers, with banners well known from the Libyan war, a proud name and a proud race. Here they turned left. The gate facing Tuscany was already called the Flaminian gate. They entered the Campus Martius ... they were shown the great temples of Minerva and that of all the gods, buildings destined for better things.

F. Petrarch, *Africa*, book VIII, lines 862–925

Petrarch was interested in inscriptions; he collected Roman coins and used them as historical evidence (of what Vespasian looked like, for example); he was interested in changes in people's clothes, and used his knowledge of Greek costume to explain a line in the *Iliad*. He was not an accurate antiquarian. In the passage from the *Africa* quoted above, he puts Caesar's palace and the Pantheon (founded by Augustus) into the Rome of Scipio Africanus! Less surprisingly, but still wrongly, he tended to follow the *Mirabilia* too closely, and to accept such traditional identifications as the 'tomb of Remus' (a pyramid in the Borgo Nuovo). His letter to Livy shows that he believed that Livy's tombstone had been found at Padua: in the seventeenth century, this was shown to be an incorrect identification. But his mistakes are not the point; what matters about Petrarch is his historical sensibility, his feeling for the past. His friends shared his interests; Cola di Rienzo, for example, who displayed a bronze inscription of Vespasian's time to a meeting and drew the conclusion that in antiquity the authority of the emperor came from the Roman people; or Giovanni Dondi, who visited Rome in 1375, copied inscriptions and made measurements. Then for some fifty years there is little trace of such antiquarian interests; they revive in the generation born in the late fourteenth century, the generation of Poggio Bracciolini 1380-1459, Cyriac of Ancona, 1381-*c.* 1455, and Flavio Biondo, 1388-1463. Poggio, meditating on the inconstancy of fortune among the ruins of Rome, goes on to list the surviving fragments – and to correct Petrarch.

The pyramid set in the walls of the city near the Porta Ostia. . . . is the noble tomb of C. Cestius, a member of the college of priests, and the letters inscribed on it refer to it as a work completed in one hundred and thirty days, from the will of Ponthus Clamela. I am the more amazed, since this inscription still survives entire, that the most learned Francesco Petrarca wrote in one of his letters that this is the tomb of Remus. . . .

> Poggio Braccioloni, 'The Inconstancy of Fortune', trans., *The Portable Renaissance Reader*, ed. J. B. Ross and M. M. McLaughlin, (1953) New York, p. 383

Cyriac of Ancona was a merchant who travelled widely in the Middle East and recorded classical inscriptions in order to bring the past to life again. As he boasted in a letter to one Johannes Ricinatus,

> It is obvious, most worthy father, that we are able by our art not only to raise from the depths monuments which have been destroyed, but also to bring the names of cities back into the light. Oh what a great, what a divine power has this art of ours:
> > Cyriac of Ancona, *Itinerarium*, ed. L. Mehus, (1742) Florence, p. 54

He wrote six volumes of commentaries, which were lost in a fire in 1514.

Still more important is Flavio Biondo, who not only inspected the ruins of Rome and copied inscriptions, but used this information in the task of historical reconstruction. His *Rome Restored* (written 1440-46) is a book of fundamental importance in the history of historical thought. It is a topographical account of ancient Rome, describing baths, temples, gates, obelisks and so on, using literary sources as well as information obtained from Biondo's own visits to the sites. Here is a selection from his section on Roman theatres, to compare with the extremely jejune account given in the *Marvels of Rome* (above, p. 2).

> The first theatre of this form (semicircular) which was seen at Rome was put up by Marcus Scaurus when he was aedile. It was not a permanent building, but was built for thirty days of plays. On this building it would be a good idea to quote Pliny, because we shall not be trusted if we make many assertions without giving evidence. 'When he was aedile he constructed the greatest building that had ever been made by human hand, counting permanent works as well as temporary ones. His theatre had a stage divided into three parts and 360 columns . . . the lowest part of the stage was of marble, the middle part was of glass, an unheard-of luxury

even in later times, and the top was of gilded planks; as we have said, it had 24 pillars . . . the auditorium held 80,000 men.' . . . in book XXXIV there are these words: 'When Marcus Scaurus was aedile there were three thousand statues on the stage of a temporary theatre.' And in book XXXVI, chapter two: 'When Marcus Scaurus was aedile, 360 columns were carried to the stage of a temporary theatre, which was to be used for scarcely a month', and below, 'the largest columns were of Lucullean marble, 38 feet long.' . . .

Writers agree that the first stone theatre was erected by Cn. Pompey, about which Cornelius Tacitus writes as follows:

*Annals*, Book XIV, chapters 20-21
'When Nero was consul for the fourth time, together with Cornelius Cossus, quinquennial games in the Greek manner were instituted at Rome out of emulation and had a mixed reception, like almost all novelties. Some said that Cn. Pompey too had been reproached by the older men for having built a permanent theatre; for before his time there were only improvised benches and a stage built for the occasion.' Later on he writes: 'one motive in building a permanent theatre was economy, not to spend an enormous amount on constructing one and demolishing it every year, and so exhaust the fortunes of the magistrates.' We cannot better demonstrate the size of this theatre than by the fact that Nero, to show the German nobles how numerous the Roman people were, so Tacitus relates, took them to the theatre of Pompey when it was full . . .

This theatre, then, was begun by Cn. Pompey and largely built by him: Suetonius writes that the emperor Caligula completed it. We know that it lasted less than 400 years, because Theodoric King of the Ostrogoths had it restored. Much of it was then in ruins . . . it is known where this theatre used to stand, but only vaguely. Among the mass of ruins near the monastery which is now called de la Rosa, the outer wing of the wall, which is bent in a circle, looks something like a theatre. However, there is better evidence that the ruins of the theatre are in fact far away from there, in the courtyard of S. Lorenzo in Damaso. The lawyer Angelo Pontano recently dug fairly deep in the wine-cellar there and found foundations in big squared stones. On one of the stones which the workmen dug up were letters a cubit high saying 'the Genius of Pompey's Theatre', so that it may be conjectured that the stone was put there when the foundation-stone was laid, which would have been made clear from the rest of the inscription ... but our opinion is that the site of the theatre was nearer S. Lorenzo itself.

> Flavio Biondo, *Rome Restored*, (1531 edition)
> Basel, pp. 257-8

In the generation after Biondo, Cyriac and Poggio, the sense of history began to affect Italian Renaissance art. For example, Piero della Francesca (*c.* 1420-92) appears to have some confused sense of anachronism in costume; his Arezzo frescoes of the life of the emperor Constantine, painted in the 1450s and 1460s, show a man in imaginatively-reconstructed Roman armour and a knight in fifteenth-century armour taking part in the same battle! A more devoted antiquary was Andrea Mantegna, 1431-1506, who was a friend of a disciple of Cyriac's, Felice Feliciano 'the antiquary' (*antiquarius*) of Verona. A document survives in which Felice describes an expedition to the Lake of Garda in 1464 to look for antiquities by a sort of club led by an 'emperor' and two 'consuls', of whom Mantegna was one. Fritz Saxl drew attention to Mantegna's picture (in the National Gallery) of the cult of Cybele being introduced to Rome by Scipio as an early example of an attempt to paint a subject from ancient history in a historically correct manner. At much the same time, the architect Antonio Filarete advised artists:

> Suit the dress to the quality of those you represent. If you have to do a thing that represents the present time, do not dress your figures in the antique fashion. In the same way, if you have to represent antiquity, do not dress them in modern dress. Do not do as many I have already seen who alter the suitability of clothing. Frequently they have given modern dress to the ancients.

> A. Filarete, *Treatise on Architecture*, book XXIV
> trans. J. Spencer, (1966) New Haven, p. 314

In England, the Warwick Rolls drawn by John Rous, 1411-91, show the same feel for period; Sir James Mann emphasised Rous's care for rendering fourteenth-century armour, for example in his drawing of Thomas Beauchamp. In his *History of the Kings of England*, Rous drew attention to such details as the introduction of exaggeratedly-pointed shoes in the late fourteenth century.

In the sixteenth century, sensivity to anachronism in costume, furnishings and so on increased. During the Counter-Reformation,

B

attempts were made by the Church to make painters more accurate in their representations of religious subjects. G. A. Gilio da Fabriano, for example, wrote a book on *The Errors of Painters* to this end, published in 1564, now most famous for its criticisms of Michelangelo. His criticisms are often pedantic: he seems to have no understanding of the symbolic function of the attributes of saints; but he is extremely, almost fanatically, aware of historical anachronism.

The prudent painter should know how to paint what is appropriate to the individual, the time and the place . . . so that he does not represent Aeneas as coming to Italy in the time of the emperor Justinian, or the battles of the Carthaginians in the presence of Pontius Pilate . . .

Another abuse that I notice is to make St. Peter decrepit at the time of the Passion of Our Lord, which seems impossible to me, seeing that there were 37 years between the Passion and the last year of Nero, in which St. Peter was crucified on the Janiculum. They also represent St. John the Evangelist invariably as a beardless boy, whereas he was 31 years old at the time of the Passion . . . Some painters can also be found who represent the Magdalen at the foot of the Cross as well turned out, perfumed, covered with jewels and golden chains, dressed in velvet and full of vanity, not realising that she was a sinner no more, but a fervent disciple of Christ. They represent St. Francis as fat and red, well-dressed, with his beard and moustache carefully combed, perfumed, with a cap of fine cloth carefully folded, with a silken cord round his waist, looking more like a general or provincial of an order than the mirror of penitence that he was; they do not realise that he wore nothing but a rough gown. The same could be said of St. Dominic, of St. Benedict, St. Bernard, and St. Romualdo. Is it not an error to paint St. Jerome with a red hat, like the one cardinals wear to-day? He was indeed a cardinal, but he did not wear such a costume, since it was Pope Innocent IV, more than 700 years later, who gave cardinals their red hats and red gowns . . . All this proceeds from the ignorance of painters. If they were educated they would not make such elementary and obvious errors.

G. A. Gilio da Fabriano, *The Errors of Painting*, (1564), reprinted in *Art Treatises*, ed. P. Barocchi, (1960-2) Bari

In the seventeenth century, Poussin (1594-1665) seems to have more

sense of the past than most painters: it extends to architecture – he looks
up Palladio to see how ancient Roman monuments once appeared; to
costume – in his *Rebecca* in the Louvre, he paints women wearing the
ancient Greek *peplos*; and even to furniture – he shows the apostles at
the Last Supper reclining on a *triclinium*.

The offspring of traditional local history and the new antiquarianism
was what men in the Renaissance called 'chorography': that is, a study
of geo-history, or a study of local history with special reference to surviving physical remains. This historical genre, known to Ptolemy in the
ancient world, was revived by Biondo, in his *Italy Illustrated* (finished
1453) which extended the approach of *Rome Restored* to the whole of
Italy, divided into its fourteen ancient regions. Here is Biondo's account of Padua, which draws both on literary and archaeological
evidence, and combines ancient with medieval and political with
architectural history, besides listing the local 'worthies'. He com-
municates a very real sense of a city as a human artefact which has
developed or changed over time.

It is well known that this most ancient and most famous city of
Italy was founded by Antenor, a fugitive from Troy ... Livy
describes the glory of the Paduans at length in his first book.
Cicero in his *Philippics* says that the Paduans were close friends of
the Romans, and helped them with money and arms in times of
trouble. Macrobius, in his *Saturnalia*, where he discusses the
loyalty of slaves, says that the Paduans were extremely humane,
treating their slaves with such clemency, and even indulgence,
that when Asinius Pollio wanted to force the Paduans to pay
tribute and they went into hiding, none of their slaves would give
them away, either in return for their freedom or for some other
reward. Q. Asconius Pedianus writes in his commentaries on the
speeches of Cicero that Padua became a Roman colony in the
golden age of the Republic; not in the normal way, by the im-
migration of new settlers, but by giving the Paduans the Latin
right, so that they could vote in the elections of magistrates at
Rome. If this description is rather long, the dignity of the city is
an excuse, for, we believe, there is nowhere like it in Italy, for the
beauty of its buildings, especially the public ones. All the buildings
that are there now, public and private, are modern, because in
430 AD Attila, king of the Huns, devastated Padua with fire and
sword and left it unfortified. Narses the eunuch and the men of
Ravenna rebuilt it, but less than a century later the Lombards

destroyed it again. In the time of Charlemagne and his descendants it grew tremendously, and did not suffer damage under the Roman emperors. However, in the time of Frederick Barbarossa, Ezzelino da Romano, the most cruel tyrant who ever lived, conquered it, in AD 1237. Besides his other atrocities, and his almost innumerable proscriptions of citizens, with unheard-of cruelty (as we said when describing Verona) he killed 12,000 Paduans in different ways, whom he had taken with him as soldiers to attack the territory of the Mantuans. Soon after Ezzelino's death near Soncino, the Carraresi became lords of Padua with the title of 'captain'. They controlled the city for more or less a hundred years, and they both enriched and beautified it. It was the Carraresi, for the most part, who built the city's triple walls, and although the river Timavo always flowed through Padua, as Livy shows in his tenth book, the Carraresi had many canals dug by hand with great labour to carry the water around the city and through the countryside for both convenience and ornament. They also had a strong castle built, and adjoining it a palace, easily the finest in Italy. They also constructed some bridges in the city itself. Henry IV, the German emperor, built the cathedral, which still exists. The palace (which, we believe, was more beautiful than any on earth), was accidentally burned down. The Venetians rebuilt it magnificently. They placed Livy's bones conspicuously on its summit.

The remarkable basilica of St. Anthony (there are very few like it in Italy) was built by the Paduans when they were half free, under the Roman Empire. At different times the citizens of Padua have built 40 parish churches and four convents for friars. In the city there is a very large church dedicated to St. Justina the virgin, 1000 paces in circumference, and surrounded by water. It is believed that this church was constructed on the ruins of an ancient building, for wherever one digs, it is possible to find most beautiful tiles. Livy's tomb[1] was discovered there in our time, and so it is permissible to think that this was the ancient temple of Jupiter in which were placed (as Livy says himself in book 10) the spoils of the Paduans' victory over the pirate Cleominos the Spartan. Today the church of St. Justina contains the relics of St. Luke the Evangelist, St. Maximus, St. Felicity, St. Matthias the apostle (the one upon whom the lot fell) and St. Prosdocimus, the patron saint of Padua. This city has five squares; the Square of the Nobles, Herb

[1] Like Petrarch, Bionde has no doubts about this

Square, Corn Square, Wood Square and Straw Square. There is a university there, the most famous in Italy, with numerous halls which help students who lack means. The teaching of Padua has produced famous men . . . There was Livy, so great a man that some nobles came from the furthest part of Spain to Rome just to see him – so writes St. Jerome, following Pliny. Paul the lawyer, celebrated in antiquity, was a Paduan. The poet Martial had two friends, poets, from Padua, Stella and Flaccus . . . Pietro d'Apono, called 'the conciliator', a man so skilled in philosophy and astronomy that he was suspected of being a magician; and Mussato and Lovato, lawyers and poets, were all citizens of Padua. Francesco Zabarella, the great lawyer, and Pileo di Prata, cardinal of the Roman church, ornamented Padua by their honour, learning, and wisdom. There was Marsilio of Padua, and, soon after him, Giovanni, Galeazzo and Gulielmo Sofilici, Giovanni Horologio, and, close behind, Antonio Cermisone, all excellent doctors.

Flavio Biondo, *Italy Illustrated*, (trans. from
1531 edition) Basel, part 9

Biondo's work was influential. It was the model for the project of the German humanist Conrad Celtis, *Germany Illustrated*, and for other works of what has been called the 'geographical Renaissance' in sixteenth-century Germany. In England it was the model for the *Britannia* of William Camden, 1551-1623. I quote a section of his description of the Sussex coast.

This castle (*Brember*) once belonged to the Braose family – King William I gave it to William de Braose, from whom the Barons of Gower and Lords of Brecknock are descended, and also the knightly family of the Shirleys, here and in Leicestershire. Of this castle only ruins now remain. Below it lies *Stening*, very busy on market-days, which in Alfred's will, if I am not mistaken, was called 'Steningham'. The ancient *Portus Adurni* was hardly three miles from here, which was a watchpost of the Romans, at the time that the Saxons began their raids on us. The port is now silted up. That *Ederington* was here, a medium-sized village which Alfred gave to his younger son, is suggested by the survival of the name almost unchanged and of the adjoining cottages now called *Portslade*, that is, 'the way to the harbour'; not to mention how easy it would be to land here, because the shore is open and flat. For the same reason, in the reign of Henry VIII, our men used to wait here for the French galleys, when they threatened our coasts, and at *Brighthelmsted*, the next day, burned one or two huts in a sudden attack.

On the next river, a little further from the sea, is *Lewes*, perhaps so-called from the pastures . . . Its size and population make it one of the chief towns of the county. It has six parish churches and a priory. Lord Buckhurst has a house there which was built by William Earl Warrenne, who also built a castle in the north part of the town, beneath which there is a ruined church, blocked up by bramble-bushes, on the walls of which are inscribed in the form of an arch some clumsy verses in an archaic form of lettering which suggest that a certain Magnus, of the Danish royal family, was buried there. Here are the verses themselves, yawning, if I may say so, with the gaps in the stones . . .

In the time of the Anglo-saxons, when Athelstan made a law forbidding money to be minted outside towns, he appointed moneyers here in two places. In Norman times there was a battle here between Henry III and his barons, which went well for the king at first – but this was his downfall. For Edward, the king's son, broke through some troops of the barons and pursued them for a long way as if the victory had already been won; the barons reassembled their forces and so defeated the royal troops so decisively that they forced the king to make peace with them on unfavourable terms and to hand over to them his son Edward and others as hostages.

W. Camden, *Britannia*, (1586) London, pp.<br>158-9

## 2   Law and the Sense of the Past

Once again, it seems impossible not to begin with Petrarch. A contemporary of Bartolus, (a great lawyer but a man without the sense of the past), Petrarch was interested in the contribution history could make to the study of law.

The greater part of our legists (he wrote), who care nothing for knowing about the origins of law and about the founders of jurisprudence, and have no other preoccupation than to gain as much as they can from their profession, are content to learn whatever is written in the law about contracts, judgements or wills, and it never occurs to them that the knowledge of arts and of origins and of literature would be of the greatest practical use for their very profession.

F. Petrarch, Letter of 1340, trans. Myron Gilmore in his *Humanists and Jurists*, (1963) Cambridge, Mass.: p. 30

As in the case of the antiquarian movement, Petrarch's idea that law had a history was not taken up and developed till towards the middle of the fifteenth century. Flavio Biondo discusses Roman law in its historical context in a third famous book of his *Rome Triumphant*. His younger friend, Lorenzo Valla, 1405-57, made a more important and a more aggressive contribution. At the age of 28, he was professor of rhetoric at Pavia when he heard someone say that Bartolus's book *Ensigns and Arms* (*De insigniis et armis*) was worth the whole of Cicero. Valla wrote a letter attacking Bartolus, which caused such a stir that he had to leave Pavia. This letter shows Valla, and humanism in general, at once at its most pedantic and its most perceptive. He attacks Bartolus as a barbarian because, for example, he wrote *de insigniis* when he should have written *de insignibus*. But then he widened his argument into the suggestion that Bartolus did not understand Roman history, Roman institutions. He suggests that one should return to the sources, to the lawyers of antiquity, to find out what they meant. Valla was primarily interested in grammar, in philology; but this interest led him to history because one can only understand the meaning of a word by looking at its context, and that context includes the mental and social world of the writer's time. Valla's friend Matteo Vegio (best known to history as the man who dared add a thirteenth book to the *Aeneid*) illustrates the positive side of Valla's programme with a little book called *The Meaning of Words* (*De verborum significatione*), an alphabetical list of Roman law terms with explanations.

It was only in the early sixteenth century that Petrarch's programme was carried further, by two great scholars, Guillaume Budé, 1468-1540, and Andrea Alciati, 1492-1550. Both were the sons of lawyers, both wrote books of 'annotations' on Roman law texts, and both taught in France: hence the name for the new historical school of law, the *mos gallicus* or 'French style', as opposed to the *mos italicus*, the manner of Bartolus, the school which still applied texts to the problems of the present without asking whether the situation was really like the one which the law had originally been devised to meet or not. In France in the sixteenth century, the historical approach to law reached what looks like its logical conclusion, the point where it was realised that, when Roman law had been put back in its historical context, that context was a society so different from that of modern France that there was no practical point in studying Roman law at all. This point was reached with François Hotman, who argued in 1567 that 'Roman law is the most useless of all studies to a modern Frenchman', and that the society (he uses the word *état*) of Republican Rome 'is quite different from that of France'.

> . . . If the study of the code of Justinian is useful, it must have some relevance to life and to the commonwealth. How can this be so in the case of laws which were made at the time of democracy and the liberty of the people, seeing that the organisation and form of a Republic is quite different from that of this Kingdom? Let us take the office of the Consuls for an example. Their duty was, together with the senate, to look after the most important affairs of the Republic; to give audience to the ambassadors of foreign nations, to hear the complaints and grievances of the provinces, to oversee finance and the financiers. Today, all these functions are performed by the King's privy council. What reason is there to make us study the laws concerning the consuls or the magistrates of the Roman republic, and to examine them so carefully, seeing that such laws are not and cannot be applied to this kingdom? We can say much the same thing about the Empire; for although it was a monarchy, as France is now, nevertheless it was a monarchy of quite a different kind. More important still, their form of government did not remain the same, but was changed, firstly during the time of the Roman Emperors, and afterwards when the seat of the Empire was moved to Constantinople . . .
>
> F. Hotman, *Anti-tribonian*, (1567) (1603 edition) Paris, pp. 15-16

The moral of this historical research was that laws have to change because circumstances change, because (as we say) societies change. This point is put very clearly by Richard Hooker *c.* 1554-1600 when he criticises the Puritans for attempting to apply Old Testament precepts to modern society. His philosophy of law is in many ways like that of Aquinas (above, p. 5) and he does quote the twelfth-century writer Gratian, but there does seem to be a new emphasis on change.

> Whether God be the author of laws by authorising that power of men whereby they are made, or by delivering them made immediately from Himself, by word only, or in writing also, or howsoever; notwithstanding the authority of their Maker, the

mutability of that end for which they are made doth also make them changeable. The law of ceremonies came from God: Moses had commandment to commit it unto the sacred records of Scripture, where it continueth even unto this very day and hour: in force still, as the Jew surmiseth, because God Himself was author of it, and for us to abolish what He hath established were presumption most intolerable. But (that which they in the blindness of their obdurate hearts are not able to discern) sith the end for which that law was ordained is now fulfilled, past and gone; how should it but cease any longer to be, which hath no longer any cause of being in force as before? 'That which necessity of some special time doth cause to be enjoined bindeth no longer than during that time, but doth afterwards become free.' (Gratian, *Decretals* 1.1.1.41)

... But such as do not stick at this point, such as grant that what hath been instituted upon any special cause needeth not be observed, that cause ceasing, do notwithstanding herein fail; they judge the laws of God only by the author and main end for which they were made, so that for us to change that which He hath established, they hold it execrable pride and presumption, if so be the end and purpose for which God by that mean provideth be permanent. And upon this they ground those ample disputes concerning orders and offices, which being by Him appointed for the government of his Church, if it be necessary always that the Church of Christ be governed, then doth the end for which God provided remain still: and therefore in those means which He did by law establish as being fittest unto that end, for us to alter any thing is to lift up ourselves against God, and as it were to countermand Him. Wherein they mark not that laws are instruments to rule by, and that instruments are not only to be framed according unto the general end for which they are provided, but even according unto that very particular, which riseth out of the matter whereon they have to work. The end wherefore laws were made may be permanent, and those laws nevertheless require some alteration, if there be any unfitness in the means which they prescribe as tending unto that end and purpose. As for example, a law that to bridle theft doth punish thieves with a quadruple restitution hath an end which will continue as long as the world itself continueth. Theft will be always, and will always need to be bridled. But that the mean which this law provideth for that end, namely the punishment of quadruple restitution, that this will be always sufficient to bridle and restrain that kind of enormity no man can warrant. Insufficiency of laws doth sometimes come by want of judgement in the makers. Which cause cannot fall into any law termed properly and immediately divine, as it may and doth unto human laws often. But that which hath been once most sufficient may wax otherwise by alteration of time and place; that punishment which hath been sometime forcible to bridle sin may grow afterwards too weak and feeble.

In a word, we plainly perceive by the difference of those three laws which the Jews received at the hands of God, the moral, ceremonial, and judicial, that if the end for which and the matter according whereunto God maketh His laws continue always one and the same, His laws also do the like; for which cause the moral law cannot be altered: secondly, that whether the matter whereon laws are made continue or continue not, if their end have once ceased, they cease also to be of force; as in the law ceremonial it fareth: finally, that albeit the end continue, as in that law of theft specified and in a great part of those ancient judicials it doth; yet forasmuch as there is not in all respects the same subject of matter remaining for which they were first instituted, even this is sufficient cause of change: and therefore laws, though both ordained of God Himself, and the end for which they were ordained continuing, may notwithstanding cease, if by alterations of persons or times they be found insufficient to attain unto that end. In which respect why may we not presume that God doth even call for such change or alteration as the very condition of things themselves doth make necessary?

> Richard Hooker, *Laws of Ecclesiastical Policy*,
> (*c.* 1592), book III, section x

I do not know whether Hooker was aware of the work of the French legal school or not. But Sir Henry Spelman, *c.* 1546–1641, certainly was. Jacques Cujas, 1520–90, and François Hotman did not confine their attention to Roman law; they also studied the law of the barbarian invaders of Europe, such as the Lombards and the Franks. In 1566, for example, Cujas edited the *Libri feudorum*. He and others, like Sir Thomas Craig, 1538–1608, author of the *Ius feudale*, became aware that the laws and social arrangements of the Middle Ages were very different from those of the Romans. They were coming to discover feudal society, as we call it now. For example, where Budé had identified them, Cujas distinguishes feudal vassals from the 'clients' of ancient Rome and elsewhere.

> I distinguish vassals from clients. It is sometimes possible to refer to vassals quite correctly as clients, but there is a clear distinction between them all the same. Clients do not have the duty of military service. It is a condition of being a vassal that one has to fight when commanded, or send a substitute, or pay a certain amount into the lord's treasury ... Clients have full ownership of their property, whereas vassals possess only the usufruct of their fiefs, whether on a temporary or a permanent basis; it is their lord who owns the fiefs ... What is a fief? It is the right of using and enjoying the property of another in perpetuity, which the owner gives on condition that the recipient be his man and perform for him military or other service.
>
> J. Cujas, *On Fiefs*, trans. from his *Works* (1658)
> Paris, volume II, columns 591-4

Spelman, for example, argues that there were no 'feuds', as he calls 'fiefs', in England before the Norman Conquest. Like Valla, he begins with philology; he notes that 'none of our Feudal words, nor words of tenure, are found in any law or ancient charter of the Saxons'. But he ends up by writing social history; by discussing the social structure of Anglo-Saxon England, and the conditions of land tenure. From the observation of changes in the meaning of words, scholars have moved to the observation of changes in law, and from that to social change.

> A Feud is a right which the Vassal hath in Land, or some immoveable thing of his Lord's, to use the same and take the profits thereof hereditarily: rendering unto his Lord such Feudal duties and services as belong to military tenure: the mere propriety [absolute ownership] of the soil always remaining unto the Lord ...
>
> It appeareth that Feuds and Tenures and the Feudal-law itself, took their original form from the Germans and Northern Nations. In such conditions therefore (how obscure soever) as Caesar and Tacitus left them to us, Gerardus Niger, the Consul of Milan (who flourished about AD 1176, and first composed them into a book) taketh them up as he there findeth them ... If we understand them to be feuds among the Saxons, or of that nature, then are we sure they were no more than for life, and not inheritable, nor stretching further, without further grace obtained from the Lord ...
>
> Let us now go on in examination, when and how Feuds became

hereditary. Some suggest a shew of such a matter under the two Othones, German Emperors, (who succeeded one the other about the year 973). But to rest upon the common and received opinion (which we shall hereafter more at large declare) the truth is, that when Hugh Capet usurped the Kingdom of France against the Carolinges he, to fortifie himself and to draw all the Nobility of France to support his Faction about the year 987, granted to them in the year 988 that whereas till then they enjoyed their Feuds and Honours but for life or at pleasure of their Princes; they should from thenceforth for ever hold them to them, and to their heirs, in Feudal manner by the Ceremony of Homage, and Oath of Fealty: and that he would accordingly maintain them therein, as they supported him and his heirs in the Crown of France; which they joyfully accepted.

This was a fair direction for William of Normandy (whom we call the Conqueror) how to secure himself of this his new ac-quired Kingdom of England; and he praetermitted [omitted] not to take the advantage of it. For with as great diligence as provi-dence, he presently transfer'd his Country-customs into England (as the Black Book of the Chequer witnesseth), and amongst them (as after shall be made perspicuous) this new French custom of making Feuds hereditary, not regarding the former use of our Saxon ancestors; who, like all other Nations, save the French, continued to that time their Feuds and Tenures, either arbitrary or in some definite limitation, according to the ancient manner of the Germans, receiv'd generally throughout Europe. For by the multitude of their Colonies and Transmigrations into all the chiefest parts thereof, they carried with them such Feodal Rites, as were then in use amongst them; and planting those Rites and Customs in those several Countries where they settled themselves, did by that means make all those several Countries to hold a general conformity in their Feuds and Military customs. So by the Longobards they were carried into Italy, by the Saliques into the Eastern parts of France, by the Franks into the West part thereof, by the Saxons into this our Britain, by their neighbours, the Western Goths, (who communicated with the Germans in Manners, Laws, and Customs) into Spain; and by the Eastern Goths into Greece itself, and the Eastern parts of Europe . . .

Sir Henry Spelman 'Feuds and Tenures', written 1639 in *Reliquiae Spelmannianae*, (1723), London, pp. 2-5

# 3   Everything has a History

During the Renaissance men became more and more conscious that
all sorts of things – buildings, clothes, words, laws – changed over time.
An early explicit statement of such an awareness is made by Chaucer
in his *Troilus and Criseyde*, *c.* 1386.

> Ye knowe ek that in forme of speche is chaunge
> Withinne a thousand yeer, and wordes tho
> That hadden pris, now wonder nyce and straunge
> Us thinketh hem, and yit thei spake hem so,
> And spedde as wel in love as men now do;
> Ek for to wynnen love in sondry ages,
> In sondry landes, sondry ben usages.
>
> ed. F. N. Robinson, (1957), Oxford, book II

Such a view of language as a historical product can be found in a more
developed form in Valla: implicit in his criticisms of the authenticity
of the Donation of Constantine (below, p. 55) and explicit in his
*Elegantiae* (The Elegance of the Latin Language) where he compares
the decline of the Roman Empire and the decline of the Latin language,
and concludes that the first caused the second.

Again, some writers began to look at the history of religion. Polydore Vergil, *c.* 1470–*c.* 1555, discussed religion, and many other subjects, in his book *On Inventors*. Sir Thomas Kendrick has called this
book a Renaissance 'Golden Bough' because Polydore was interested
in possible pagan origins of Christian ritual. He is fascinated by the
questions of when and why religion started, and he has some conception of social history; he is aware of the political importance of the
coming of agriculture.

> There is no doubt that men, who before agriculture lived with-
> out any ruler, began to honour their first kings and praise them
> so much that, inspired by devils, they called them gods. Perhaps
> this was on account of their outstanding virtues, or, as is custom-
> ary, to flatter them, or in thanksgiving for benefits received. Just
> as kings were loved by their subjects, so posterity remembered
> them with affection. Men made images of their kings in order to
> have the pleasure of looking at them; soon they began to worship
> them as gods, more especially to encourage virtue – for every
> good man would take risks for the commonwealth more willingly,
> if he knew that the memory of brave men was consecrated by
> honour from the immortal gods. In this way (as St. Cyprian ex-

plains in his book *On idols*) a false religion came into existence little by little – parents taught their children these observances, and they taught their children, and so on. So, in the days of Jupiter (according to Lactantius, book 2, chapter 11), the first temples were built, and a new cult of the gods began; or perhaps it was a little before. For it is possible, as he says, that before Jupiter's time, or when he was a boy, Melissus, who brought him up (from whom, as we shall point out below, all religious ceremonies originated), began to worship his charge's mother, and his grandmother, Earth, and his father, Saturn. He was three hundred and twenty-two years before the Trojan War. Belus is also said to have lived at this time whom the Babylonians and Assyrians worshipped – my authority is Theophilus in his book *On Times*, written to Autolicus. So those who argue that the worship of the gods existed from the beginning of time, are wrong . . . it was the Egyptians (according to Herodotus, book 2, and Strabo, *Geography*, book 17) who first built altars, shrines and images for the gods, and offered sacrifices to them, and then taught these ceremonies to others.

> Polydore Vergil, *On Inventors*, (1499) Venice,
> book 1, chapter 5

In the early sixteenth century, the idea spread that the Church of Rome had departed from the practice of the primitive Church, and that it would be good to return to the origins. The Anabaptists preached fundamentalism – literal adherence to Biblical commands, in every detail. Luther and Calvin were more selective, and wanted a return to the spirit of the Gospels and the Epistles of St. Paul. In both its forms, this central idea of the Reformation illustrates the new sense of history, for it implies an awareness that the Church has changed over time. Of course the reformers also thought that it would be possible to go back to the primitive Church, a view we might find 'unhistorical' – but that is a separate point. Here is Calvin on what one might call the 'constitutional history' of the Church, arguing from early Church history.

Up till now we have spoken of the order of governing the Church as it has been left to us by the word of God alone: we have also discussed ministers as they were instituted by Jesus Christ. Now that all this has been discussed and is printed on our memory, it will be useful to treat of the practice of the primitive Church (*Église Ancienne*), in these matters, for it can show us as in a mirror the reflection of that divine plan which we have been discussing. For although the ancient bishops made many canons or rules, so that it seems clear that they carried organisation much further than had been laid down by God in Scripture, nevertheless their discipline and government was so closely related to God's word, that it is easy to see that they did not differ from it in any way . . .

The freedom to choose bishops was long left to the people, and no one was made a bishop unless everyone approved of him. At the Council of Antioch it was forbidden for anyone to be ordained bishop against the will of the people. Leo I confirmed this, declaring that the candidate to be chosen was the one put forward by the clergy and the common people, or at least by a majority of them. Again, the pope said that the man who presides over everyone should be chosen by everyone; a man who is ordained without being known and examined is introduced by force. Again, he said that the man whom the clergy and people wanted should be chosen, and consecrated by the bishops of the province with the authorisation of the metropolitan. The holy fathers were so anxious for this liberty of the people not to be infringed, that even the general council assembled at Constantinople did not want to ordain Nectarius bishop, without the approval of the clergy and people, as appears from the letter sent to the bishop of Rome. . . .

> Jean Calvin, *Institutes of the Christian Religion*,
> (1560 edition), book IV, chapter 4

Another interesting illustration of Calvin's historical awareness comes from his attack on false relics, where he discusses Christ's robe, which the soldiers took from him.

The most priceless thing is that they display not only the robe but also the dice which the soldiers used to cast lots for it. One is at Trier, and two others at Saint Salvador in Spain. In this matter they have made their foolishness quite plain; for the Evangelists say that the soldiers drew lots, which used then to be drawn from a hat or a jar, just as when one chooses a Twelfth-Night king, or when one plays 'la blanque'.[1] In short, they drew lots, as is often done when there is a shareout. These fools have imagined that the soldiers were playing dice, a game which was not customary then, at least not in the form in which we know it; for instead of the 6, and the 1, and the other numbers, they had certain signs to which they gave names like 'Venus' or 'Dog'.

> Jean Calvin, *Treatise on Relics*, (1543) (1962 edition) Paris, p. 58

[1] A 16th-century lottery

Like religion, art was seen to have a history; the Renaissance view of its own art as a return to antiquity after an age of barbarism and the 'Greek manner' implies this. A classic statement of the idea that art has a history, that it can be divided into periods, and that it progresses, is provided by Giorgio Vasari, 1512–74.

> Having set out to write the history of distinguished artists in order to honour them and to benefit the arts to the best of my ability, I have tried as far as I could to imitate the methods of the great historians. I have endeavoured not only to record what the artists have done but also to distinguish between the good, the better, and the best, and to note with some care the methods, manners, styles, behaviour, and ideas of the painters and sculptors. I have tried as well as I know how to help people who cannot find out for themselves to understand the sources and origins of various styles and the reasons for the improvement or decline of the arts at various times and among different people ... I have divided the artists into three sections or, shall we say, periods, each with its own recognisably distinct character, running from the time of the rebirth of the arts up to our own times.
>
> In the first and oldest period the three arts evidently fell a long way short of perfection and, although they may have shown some good qualities, were accompanied by so much that was imperfect that they certainly do not deserve a great deal of praise. All the same, they did mark a new beginning, opening the way for the better work which followed; and if only for this reason I have to speak in their favour and to allow them rather more distinction than the work of that time would deserve if judged by the strict rules of art.
>
> Then in the second period there was clearly a considerable improvement in invention and execution, with more design, better style, and a more careful finish; and as a result artists cleaned away the rust of the old style, along with the stiffness and disproportion characteristic of the ineptitude of the first period. Even so, how can one claim that in the second period there was one artist perfect in everything, producing works comparable in invention, design and colouring to those of today? Who at that time rendered his figures with the shadows softly darkened in, so that the lights remain only on the parts in relief, and who achieved the perforations and various superb finishings seen in the marble statues executed today?

These achievements certainly belong to the third period, when I can confidently say that art has achieved everything possible in the imitation of nature, and has progressed so far that it has more reason to fear slipping back than to expect ever to make further advances.

Having very carefully turned all this over in my mind, I have come to the conclusion that it is inherent in the very nature of these arts to progress step by step from modest beginnings, and finally to reach the summit of perfection. And I believe this is so from having seen almost the same progression in other branches of learning; the fact that the liberal arts are all related to each other in some way is a persuasive argument for what I am saying.

> G. Vasari, *Lives*, (1550), preface to part 2, trans.
> G. Bull, (1965) London

With his last remark, Vasari points the way to a complete cultural history. He is also aware that standards have changed, so that all the more credit is due to Cimabue and Arnolfo di Cambio, because of the time of 'darkness' in which they lived. At one point a doctrine of historical relativism becomes explicit in Vasari.

> To those to whom it might appear that I have overpraised any craftsmen, whether old or modern, and who, comparing the old with those of the present age, might laugh at them, I know not what else to answer save that my intention has always been to praise not absolutely, but, as the saying is, relatively (*non semplicemente ma, como s'usa dire, secondo chè*) having regard to place, time, and other similar circumstances.

> G. Vasari, *Lives*, (1550), trans. in E. Panofsky,
> *Meaning in the Visual Arts*, (1955) New York,
> p. 212

It was not long before writers appeared to do for literature what Vasari had done for art. For French literature a progress-theory was put forward by Étienne Pasquier, 1529–1615.

> The arts and sciences have their revolutions and their breaks in continuity, like everything else, and travel from some countries to others. We had been wallowing in ignorance for a long time when, under Louis VII and his son Philip Augustus, literature (*les bonnes lettres*) began to awaken. In Latin poetry we had Leoninus and Gualterus, who wrote the *Alexandreid* in Latin; and French poetry

began to spring to life as well . . . from the time of Philip Augustus to that of Philip the Handsome, we had an infinity of poets, among whom I find that Pierre de St. Cloud and Jean li Nevelois had a greater reputation than the rest . . . everything changes from one period to another (*selon la diversité des temps*) and so after our French poetry had lain fallow for long years, some new fruits began to appear on its old stem, fruits unknown to all our ancient poets; these were *chants royaux, ballades* and *rondeaux* . . . these *chants royaux, ballades, rondeaux* and *pastorales* began to be written at about the time of Charles V, in whose reign the whole kingdom was rich and flourishing, and at the same time literature began to revive. He held literature in such high esteem that he asked Master Nicole Oresme to translate the greater part of the works of Aristotle into French and made him bishop of Lisieux. The man who seems to me to have done a great deal for this new poetry was Jean Froissart, who also made us a present of that long history which he wrote about the period from Philip of Valois to the year 1400. It astonishes me that he was not praised as a poet in former times, for once I saw a great volume of his poetry in the library of the great king Francis at Fontainebleau . . . the first man to make our poetry fashionable with good reason was Master Jean Lemaire des Belges, to whom we are infinitely indebted, not only for his book on the fame of the Gauls, but also for having greatly enriched our language in both prose and poetry with an infinite number of turns of phrase which have been taken over on occasion by the best writers of our time . . . On the death of Louis XII, the great Francis succeeded, the first of that name, who was the restorer of literature, and his example stimulated an infinite number of talented people to follow him, in the field of French poetry among others, among whom Clement Marot and Mellin de St.-Gelais were the most important . . . all those of whom I have spoken were like a nursery, which was entered by some other great poets in the reign of Henry II. These men claimed from the start to write for themselves rather than to please the common people. The first to cross the threshold was Maurice Scève of Lyons . . . There was now a great war on ignorance, and the vanguard of the army was Scève, Bèze, and Pelletier, or, if you prefer another image, these were the forerunners of the other poets. After them marched Pierre de Ronsard, a Vendomois, and Joachim du Bellay, an Angevin . . . After the death of King Henry, the religious wars in France troubled the waters of the fountain of

Parnassus, but all the same our spirits revived little by little and now we do not lack good poets . . .

E. Pasquier, *Researches on France*, (1611) Paris, book vii

In England, Richard Puttenham, *c.* 1520-*c.* 1601, in his *The Art of English Poesie*, put forward a similar view of progress in English literature, from Chaucer to Wyatt and Surrey. In France, Lancelot Voisin de la Popelinière, 1540-1608, wrote *The History of Histories* (1599), the first book on the history of history. And Francis Bacon, 1561-1626, summed up the whole trend towards the rise of what we would call 'cultural history' with his famous manifesto about the importance and the method of writing the history of learning, and the arts.

Civil History may rightly be divided into three species. First, Sacred or Ecclesiastical; next, that which we call Civil History (using the generic name specially); lastly, the History of Learning and the Arts. I will begin with the kind last-mentioned; for the two former are extant, while the latter – the History of Learning – (without which the history of the world seems to me as the statue of Polyphemus without the eye; that very feature being left out which most marks the spirit and life of the person), I set down as wanting. Not but I know that in the particular sciences of the jurisconsults, mathematicians, rhetoricians, philosophers, we have some slight mention or some barren narrations about the sects, schools, books, authors, and successions belonging to them; also that there exist some meagre and unprofitable memoirs of the inventors of arts and usages; but I say that a complete and universal History of Learning is yet wanting. Of this therefore I will now proceed to set forth the argument, the method of construction, and the use.

The argument is no other than to inquire and collect out of the records of all time what particular kinds of learning and arts have flourished in what ages and regions of the world; their antiquities, their progresses, their migrations (for sciences migrate like nations) over the different parts of the globe; and again their decays, disappearances, and revivals. The occasion and origin of the invention of each art should likewise be observed; the manner and system of transmission, and the plan and order of study and practice. To these should be added a history of the sects, and the principal controversies in which learned men have been engaged, the calumnies to which they have been exposed, the praises and honours by which they have been rewarded; an account of the principal authors, books, schools, successions, academies, societies, colleges, orders, – in a word, everything which relates to the state of learning. Above all things (for this is the ornament and life of Civil History), I wish events to be coupled with their causes. I mean, that an account should be given of the characters of the several regions and peoples; their natural disposition, whether apt and suited for the study of learning, or unfitted and indifferent to it; the accidents of the times, whether adverse or propitious to science; the emulations and infusions of different religions; the enmity or partiality of laws; the eminent virtues and services of individual persons in the promotion of learning, and the like. Now all this I would have handled in a historical way, not wasting time, after the manner of critics, in praise and blame, but simply narrating the fact historically, with but slight intermixture of private judgment.

For the manner of compiling such a history I particularly advise that the matter and provision of it be not drawn from histories and commentaries alone; but that the principal books written in each century, or perhaps in shorter periods, proceeding in regular order from the earliest ages, be themselves taken into consultation; that so (I do not say by a complete perusal, for that would be an endless labour, but) by tasting them here and there, and observing their argument, style, and method, the Literary Spirit of each age may be charmed as it were from the dead.

With regard to the use of the work, it is not so much to swell the honour and pomp of learning with a profusion of images; nor because out of my exceeding love for learning I wish the inquiry, knowledge, and preservation of everything that relates thereto to be pursued even to curiosity; but chiefly for a purpose more serious and important; which, in a word, is this: I consider that such a history as I have described, would very greatly assist the wisdom and skill of learned men in the use and administration of learning; that it would exhibit the movements and perturbations, the virtues and vices, which take place no less in intellectual than in civil matters; and that from the observation of these the best system of government might be derived and established. For the works of St. Ambrose or St. Augustine will not make so wise a bishop or divine as a diligent examination and study of Ecclesiastical History; and the History of Learning would be of like service to learned men. For everything is subject to chance and error which is not supported by examples and experience. And so much for the History of Learning.

F. Bacon, *De Augmentis*, (1623), trans. J. Spedding, book II, chapter 4

Another example of the heightened sense of the past in the fifteenth, sixteenth and seventeenth centuries is the great interest that was taken in questions of chronology. The great problem was how to harmonise Biblical chronology with the chronologies of the other nations of antiquity. In this field the great landmark is a book by Joseph Justus Scaliger, 1540-1609. It is called the *Reform of Chronology* (*De emendatione temporum*) and was published at Paris in 1583. It was lavishly illustrated with tables, and it drew on recent astronomical as well as historical research, using the records of other nations besides the Greeks, Romans and the Jews. Scaliger reduced all chronologies to a new one, the Julian, which was a period of 7980 years derived by combining the solar cycle (28 years) – the lunar cycle (19 years) and the cycle of the indiction (a 15-year cycle of no astronomical significance). He began his chronology in 4713 B.C., a year when the three cycles coincided and a year before any historical events then known. His work was criticised by two Jesuits; by Clavius, the astronomer, who wrote a refutation of Scaliger's 'cyclometry', as he called it; and by Petavius in his book *On Chronology* (1627). A third Jesuit, Juan de Mariana, 1535-1625, better known today for his political theory, wrote on specific chronological problems, such as the exact date of Christ's death, and the differences between European and Arab systems of chronology. In Britain, the great contribution to this subject was made by James Ussher, 1581-1656, the archbishop of Armagh, a famous scholar who was particularly interested in early Church and early Irish history. He published his *Annals of the Old Testament* in 1650. His epistle to the reader explains his ambition:

If anyone well seen in the knowledge not only of sacred and exotic [i.e. secular] history, but of astronomical calculation, and the old Hebrew calendar, should apply himself to these studies, I judge it indeed difficult, but not impossible, for such a one to attain, not only the number of years, but even of days from the creation of the world . . .

His conclusion about the date of the world's creation has become celebrated for the naiveté with which he dates the 'beginning of time'.

In the beginning, God created Heaven and Earth, Genesis 1. verse 1. Which beginning of time, according to our chronologers, fell upon the entrance of the night preceding the 23rd day of October in the year of the Julian Calendar, 710 ... [Marginal note: the year before Christ, 4004]. On the second day (October 24, being Monday) the firmament being finished, which was called Heaven, a separation was made of the waters above, and the waters here beneath enclosing the earth.

J. Ussher, *Annals of the Old and New Testament*,
(1650), from the 1658 trans., p. 1

However, Ussher, like Petavius and Scaliger, should be given credit for his use of astronomical data, not handled with ease by many historians; for his study of Egyptian and Asian history; and for his denial of the traditional date of Christ's birth and suggestion that, as Ussher puts it,

the true nativity of our Saviour was full four years before the beginning of the vulgar Christian era.

The study of chronology is the most technical aspect of the new sense of the past. To conclude the chapter, I should like to turn to the sensibility of the ordinary educated man of about the year 1600. The work of the scholars discussed in this chapter had had the effect, by this time, of making men aware of many ways in which the past was unlike the present; more particularly the classical past. This awareness found expression in literature. Ben Jonson, the friend of such historians as Camden and Selden, and himself a man keenly interested in history, tried to make his Roman plays really Roman. For example, in *Sejanus* he introduced a Roman religious rite, addressed to Fortune:

*A chapel in Sejanus's house.*
*Enter* Praecones, Tubicines, Tibicines, Flamen, Ministri, Sejanus, Terentius, Satrius, Natta, etc.
*Prae.* Be all profane far hence; Fly fly far off:
Be absent far. Far hence be all profane.
                    (Tub. Tib. *sound while the* Flamen *washeth.*)
*Fla.* We have been faulty but repent us now,
And bring pure hands, pure vestments, and pure minds.
1 *Min.* Pure vessels
2 *Min.*                    And pure offerings.
3 *Min.*                                        Garlands pure.

*Fla.* Bestow your garlands: and, with reverence, place
The vervin on the altar.
*Prae.*                              Favour your tongues.
*While they sound again, the* Flamen *takes of the honey with his finger and tastes, then ministers to all the rest: so of the milk in an earthen vessel, he deals about: which done, he sprinkleth, upon the altar, milk: then imposeth the honey, and kindleth his gums, and after censing about the altar placeth his censer thereon, into which they put several branches of poppy, and, the music ceasing, proceeds.*
*Fla.* Great mother Fortune, Queen of human state,
Rectress of action, arbitress of fate,
To whom all sway, all power, all empire bows,
Be present, and propitious to our vows.

> Ben Jonson, *Sejanus* (première 1603), act
> V. scene IV.

Shakespeare was much less interested in getting the details right than Jonson, but in his Roman plays he does communicate a sense of what it felt like to have values which were not English or Christian but Roman and stoic; suicide as a noble act, for example. This sympathetic awareness of different values in a different period owes a great deal, not only to Shakespeare's genius, but also to the Renaissance sense of history. It is the literary equivalent of Poussin's feeling for the appearance of classical antiquity.

# III

# SOURCES AND SCEPTICISM

During the Renaissance, scholars became better able to tell good sources from bad ones. This increased awareness of evidence is shown most spectacularly in the cases of the exposure of certain documents as forgeries, and of certain beliefs as myths, though it can also be found in the reinterpretation of texts, the careful editing of important sources, and in simple historical narrative.

## 1   The Criticism of Documents

Here once more it seems impossible not to start with Petrarch, who was asked by the Emperor Charles IV to give his opinion about the authenticity of a document which claimed to exempt 'Austria' from his jurisdiction. This example, like the ones which follow, shows how closely connected are the sense of anachronism and the awareness of evidence; it is because of its many anachronisms that Petrarch decides that the privilege is a forgery. It should be noticed that Petrarch employs the devices of both internal and external criticism.

*Francesco Petrarca to the Roman Emperor Charles IV* (1355)
On the false privilege exempting Austria from imperial jurisdiction. Lies always limp and are easily caught. It is difficult for them to escape the verdict of a keen, quick intellect. This morning I saw a manuscript which was full of words and empty of truth. I do not know who wrote it, but have no doubt that he was not a learned man but a schoolboy, an ignorant writer, a man with the desire to lie but without the skill to do it properly – otherwise he would not have made such stupid mistakes. Forgers usually give their falsehoods some colour of truth, so that it is possible to believe what never happened, because it is similar to things which did happen.

The author – it is utter madness – seems to have believed that with this trifle he could overthrow Roman law and the Empire too, defended as it is by arms, laws, and virtues. He might at least have produced more workmanlike lies, which did not look false even to the almost blind.

I have no doubt Caesar, that the whole of this rascal's deceit was immediately apparent to you, and to your nobles, wise and learned men, and especially to your lynx-eyed chancellor. However, you ask me for an opinion too. I shall tell you the first impression it made on me, busy and anxious as I am. It is no small honour that Your Highness wanted me to be a party to the secret and considered me the right man to expose these deceits.

I shall not discuss the point that no one has authority over his equals, and that Julius Caesar and Nero did not make any decree which you have not the right to reverse. The rogue did not realise this when he pretended, with clumsy cunning, that they were the authors of that disgraceful privilege, as if what the best of princes had decreed, and the worst had confirmed, could not be revoked by anyone. I leave this question to your lawyers, or better still, to you, since, (as I learned in the law-schools when I was young), you contain all laws within yourself.

I come now to the point you are waiting for. 'We', he says, 'the emperor Julius Caesar, we, Caesar, worshipper of the gods, lord of the land, the imperial Augustus,' etc. Who is so stupid or so ignorant that he cannot see that there are almost as many lies here as there are words? Although (as Lucan says) this dishonest plural had long been used to address great men, they did not yet use it themselves. So, although his flattering followers had begun to speak to Caesar as if he were plural, which was never done to anyone before him (a custom which later became a general one), he himself, speaking to his troops, always referred to himself in the singular. That ox did not know this fact, or he would have bellowed more warily.

I own a number of Julius Caesar's personal letters. His speeches, many of which are to be found in the works of Lucan and other writers, and one in Sallust, were not composed by him, but by those writers themselves. But he dictated his letters in person. Here is an example.

'Caesar to Oppius and Cornelius, greetings. I am most glad to learn from your letters that you approve completely of what was done at Confinium. I should be glad of your advice, all the more because I plan to do something that I scarcely approve of myself.'

Again:

'Caesar to Oppius and Cornelius, greetings. On the seventh day before the Ides of March I came to Brundisium and pitched camp near its walls. Pompey is at Brundisium; he sent Gn. Magius to me to discuss peace. I replied as we planned; I wanted you to know at once. When there is hope of an agreement, I will tell you immediately.'

Again, writing to Cicero:

'Although I know that you are not afraid, I do not believe that you will do anything imprudent either. But being worried by rumours, I thought I should write to you,' etc.

There exists a letter of his, or rather a decree, concerning an important matter, addressed not to individual friends but to the people of Sidon, as follows:

'G. Julius Caesar, general (*imperator*) and pontifex, and dictator for the second time, to the magistrates and people of Sidon and Cinthia, greetings. If you are well, it is good; my army and I are well. I have sent you a copy of the decree to Hircanus, son of Alexander the chief priest and ruler of the Jews, to be inserted in your public annals. I want this decree to be written on bronze in Greek and Latin. Immediately afterwards, I decreed that Hircanus and the sons of Alexander should be the rulers of the Jewish people and should always be their high-priests, according to the customs of their ancestors. I order that he and his sons should be counted among our allies and our very good friends, and that they should have all the rights of the high priest', etc.

If you want this letter, you will find it in the third book of Josephus, a most reliable author. I could give more examples: you see his style. Who does not see not only how false, but also how ridiculous it is that Julius Caesar should call himself Augustus! I thought that every schoolboy knew that that name began to be used by his successor. Read Florus, read Suetonius, read Orosius, read Eutropius, in fact read all the historians. Everyone knows, except this ass who is now braying so inappropriately.

I do not understand what follows, what invented uncle this is, something quite extraordinary, known only in these scribblings and found nowhere else; especially odd in that little or nothing is known of Caesar's father even. I would be surprised at this if I were not accustomed to believing this man's glory to be so great, his name so illustrious, that those around him paled beside him like the stars beside the sun. I do not know where this uncle sprang from, or where he was hiding for so many centuries, or for what offence he was taken to the ends of the earth. I am extremely surprised that an anonymous witness is brought into the case, and in such a great matter trust is placed in one whose name is as doubtful as his testimony. The privilege is also invalid because it lacks the name of the man to whom it was made, since privileges (as I learned when I was a boy), are of restricted application. There are many things here which weaken it, but this matter I leave to your lawyers.

Nor is it possible to argue seriously that what is called 'Austria' is an eastern region. 'Auster' (South) and 'Oriens' (East) are different. They are names for the directions of different regions, directions which vary with one's own position. From Rome, from the city from which the document claims to come, which removes this region, Austria, from imperial jurisdiction, Austria is not south, but north.

The date of the document is clearly false. It does not indicate the exact day, nor the consuls in office. Only an idiot would say 'given at Rome on Friday in the first year of our reign' without adding the month and the day. What shepherd, what ploughman would write like this – let alone the man who had, besides his other great deeds, reformed the calendar! Then he says 'of our reign', which is so far from the truth as to arouse indignation as well as laughter. For, as you have heard, Caesar wished to be called 'general' (*imperator*), 'pontifex', and 'dictator' – never 'king' (*rex*). We read that Rome in earliest times had seven kings. Those who wished to become kings after this were put to the sword or thrown from the rock on the Capitol hill. I admit that Caesar was suspected of wishing to be king – but only by his enemies. He was too prudent and too careful of his reputation to take a title which would have made him infamous. He would no more call himself a 'king' (or allow himself to be called one) than 'buffoon', 'adulterer' or 'pimp'. In fact he was even less likely to allow it, for while the other names are shameful and filthy, that of 'king' was odious, dangerous and intolerable at Rome. Here is the evidence.

When the Spanish people offered Scipio Africanus the title of 'king' out of admiration for his great and glorious achievements, look at what he answered. I quote Livy's own words. 'After the

herald had made silence, he said that his greatest title was that of
"general" (*imperator*), which his soldiers had given him. The name
of "king" was a great one elsewhere, but at Rome it was not toler-
ated.' And so Lucan said 'Caesar was everything,' meaning that
he united in himself all the honours of Rome, where there was
no royal title. Caesar could not have mentioned his 'reign': had
he done so he would have been execrated and rejected.

This is my answer to that ignorant and clumsy fabricator of lies
concerning his stories about Julius Caesar. Much of it is also
applicable to what he says about Nero, ending 'given on the day
of the great god Mars'. [Tuesday]. Oh shameless, stupid man!
How will you answer critics? What Monday and what Wednes-
day precede and follow this day? Who can tolerate this wild lying,
this foolishness?

Caesar, you may laugh and be glad that the rebels against you
are able to do you less harm than they would like; they attack
your authority and claim their liberty on the basis of more lies than
they realise. If they had, he would never have begun with a lie
like this: 'We, Nero, the friend of the gods', when we read that
he despised all the gods; for Suetonius says of him in Book VI of
his *Lives of the Caesars*, 'He always had contempt for religion,
except one, that of the goddess Syria. But he soon despised her
enough to [sully her image].'

These, oh emperor, are my immediate comments without a
detailed study. I omit the question of the style of both letters,
which from beginning to end is both barbarous and modern. It is
clear that these documents were thrown together quite recently in
a childish attempt to imitate the style of the ancients. It is impossible not to see the falsehood, which is apparent in every word.
The whole thing is so different from what the forger aimed at, so
remote from antiquity and the style of Caesar, that a credulous old
woman or a mountain peasant might perhaps be taken in, but
certainly not a man of intelligence.

You have sent me a letter dictated in anger. I much approve of
its style and rejoice that praise is due to you not only as a soldier
and a judge, but as a writer too.

Caesar, farewell. Be mindful of me and of the empire, and lead
a life such that your friends do not lie to you and your enemies
fear you.

Milan, the 12th before the Kalends of April, in haste.

F. Petrarch, *Works*, (1554) Basel, pp. 1055-8

A second example of scepticism. Coluccio Salutati, humanist and follower of Petrarch, in a letter of 1401 refers to the histories of Dares and Dictys as apocryphal, though he does not undertake to expose them.

The most famous of all exposures of forged documents is that of the Donation of Constantine (above, p. 12). Towards the middle of the fifteenth century, this document was suddenly seen to be a forgery. The point was made independently by Nicholas of Cusa, Reginald Pecock, and Lorenzo Valla, not to mention less famous scholars. This simultaneity suggests that the new sense of history was spreading. Nicholas of Cusa, 1401-64, in his book *On Catholic Harmony* pointed out that the Donation is not mentioned by St. Jerome, St. Augustine, or St. Ambrose, and that the emperors acted as overlords of Rome until the eighth century. He does not, however, criticise the document internally. Reginald Pecock, *c.* 1395-*c.* 1460, Bishop of Chichester, gave eight reasons for believing the Donation to be a forgery: here is one of them.

> The iije. principal euydence is this: if eny such now seid endewing was mad by Constantyn, sum mensioun schulde haue be made therof in sum fundamental and credible stori or cronicle. But so it is, that of thilk endewing no stori or cronicle makith mensioun, saue the legende or storie of Siluestris gestis and the oon bifore seid epistle putt and ascryued vnlikeli to Constantyn, and tho stories and cronicles which taken of it and fol ewen it; and neither thilk storiyng of Siluestris gestis neither the seid epistle is not credible neither worthi be allowid, as it is schewid bifore in the next chapiter, and as schal better be cleer aftir in this present chapiter. Wherfore it is not to be takun and to be trowid as a trouthe, that Constantyn made eny such seid so greet endewing.
>
> R. Pecock, *The Repressor of Overmuch Blaming of the Clergy*, (1455), ed. C. Babington, (1860) London, volume II, p. 361

However, the classic exposure of the Donation was that made by Lorenzo Valla in 1439. His is the most elaborate and systematic criticism, and it is based both on internal and external evidence. His attack on the Donation clearly demonstrates how closely philology and the sense of history are connected.

> Let us talk to this sycophant about barbarisms of speech; for by the stupidity of his language his monstrous impudence is made clear, and his lie.

'We give,' he says, 'our imperial Lateran palace': as though it was awkward to place the gift of the palace here among the ornaments, he repeated it later where gifts are treated. 'Then the diadem;' and as though those present would not know, he interprets, 'that is, the crown.' He did not, indeed, here add 'of gold', but later, emphasising the same statements, he says, 'of purest gold and precious gems'. The ignorant fellow did not know that a diadem was made of coarse cloth or perhaps of silk; whence that wise and oft-repeated remark of the king, who, they say, before he put upon his head the diadem given him, held it and considered it long and exclaimed, 'O cloth more renowned than happy! If any one knew you through and through, with how many anxieties and dangers and miseries you are fraught, he would not care to pick up; no, not even if you were lying on the ground!' This fellow imagines that it is of gold, with a gold band and gems such as kings now usually add. But Constantine was not a king, nor would he have dared to call himself king, nor to adorn himself with royal ceremony. He was Emperor of the Romans, not king. Where there is a king, there is no republic. But in the republic there were many, even at the same time, who were *imperatores* [generals]; for Cicero frequently writes thus, 'Marcus Cicero, imperator, to some other imperator, greeting': though, later on, the Roman ruler, as the highest of all, is called by way of distinctive title the Emperor.

'And at the same time the tiara and also the shoulder-band – that is the strap that usually surrounds our imperial neck'. Who ever heard 'tiara' [*phrygium*] used in Latin? You talk like a barbarian and want it to seem to me to be a speech of Constantine's or of Lactantius'. Plautus, in the Menaechmi, applied 'phrygionem' to a designer of garments; Pliny calls cloths embroidered with a needle 'phrygiones' because the Phrygians invented them; but what does 'phrygium' mean? You do not explain this, which is obscure; you explain what is quite clear. You say the 'shoulder-band' is a 'strap', and you do not perceive what the strap is, for you do not visualise a leather band, which we call a strap, encircling the Caesar's neck as an ornament. [It is of leather], hence we call harness and whips 'straps': but if ever gold straps are mentioned, it can only be understood as applying to gild harness such as is put around the neck of a horse or of some other animal. But this has escaped your notice, I think. So when you wish to put a strap around the Caesar's neck, or Sylvester's, you change a man, an Emperor, a supreme pontiff, into a horse or an ass. 'And also the purple mantle and scarlet tunic.' Because Matthew says 'a scarlet robe', and John 'a purple robe', this fellow tries to join them together in the same passage. But if they are the same color, as the Evangelists imply, why are you not content, as they were, to name either one alone; unless, like ignorant folk today, you use 'purple' for silk goods of a whitish color? The 'purple' (*purpura*) however, is a fish in whose blood wool is dyed, and so from the dye the name has been given to the cloth, whose color can be called red, though it may rather be blackish and very nearly the color of clotted blood, a sort of violet. Hence by Homer and Virgil blood is called purple, as is porphyry, the color of which is similar to amethyst; for the Greeks call purple 'porphyra.' You know perhaps that scarlet is used for red; but I would swear that you do not know at all why he makes it 'coccineum' when we say 'coccum' or what sort of a garment a 'mantle' [*chlamys*] is.

But that he might not betray himself as a liar by continuing longer on the separate garments, he embraced them all together in a single word, saying, 'all the imperial raiment'. What! even that which he is accustomed to wear in war, in the chase, at banquets, in games? What could be more stupid than to say that all the raiment of the Caesar befits a pontiff!

But how gracefully he adds, 'and the same rank as those presiding over the imperial cavalry'. He says 'seu' ['or' for 'and']. He wishes to distinguish between these two in turn, as if they were very like each other, and slips along from the imperial raiment to the equestrian rank, saying – I know not what! He wants to say something wonderful, but fears to be caught lying, and so with puffed cheeks and swollen throat, he gives forth sound without sense.

'Conferring also on him the imperial sceptres'. What a turn of speech! What splendor! What harmony! What are these imperial sceptres? There is one sceptre, not several; if indeed the Emperor carried a sceptre at all. Will now the pontiff carry a sceptre in his hand? Why not give him a sword also, and helmet and javelin?

'And at the same time all the standards and banners'. What do you understand by 'standards' [*signa*]? 'Signa' are either statues (hence frequently we read 'signa et tabulas' for pieces of sculpture and paintings; – for the ancients did not paint on walls, but on tablets) or military standards (hence that phrase 'Standards, matched eagles'). In the former sense small statues and sculptures are called 'sigilla'. Now then, did Constantine give Sylvester his statues or his eagles? What could be more absurd? But what 'banners' [*banna*] may signify, I do not discover. May God destroy you, most depraved of mortals who attribute barbarous language to a cultured age!

'And different imperial ornaments'. When he said 'banners' he thought he had been explicit long enough, and therefore he lumped the rest under a general term. And how frequently he drives home the word 'imperial', as though there were certain ornaments peculiar to the Emperor over against the consul, the dictator, the Caesar!

'And all the pomp of our imperial eminence, and the glory of our power'. 'He discards bombast and cubit-long words,' 'This king of kings, Darius, the kinsman of the gods', never speaking save in the plural! What is this imperial 'pomp'; that of the cucumber twisted in the grass, and growing at the belly? Do you think the Caesar celebrated a triumph whenever he left his house, as the Pope now does, preceded by white horses which servants lead saddled and adorned? To pass over other follies, nothing is emptier, more unbecoming a Roman pontiff than this. And what is this 'glory'? Would a Latin have called pomp and paraphernalia 'glory', as is customary in the Hebrew language? And instead of 'soldiers' [*milites*] you say soldiery [*militia*] which we have borrowed from the Hebrews, whose books neither Constantine nor his secretaries ever laid eyes on!

> L. Valla, *Donation of Constantine*, slightly adapted from trans. by C. B. Coleman, (1922) New Haven, pp. 105f

If any one man is of crucial importance in the development of awareness of literary evidence and criticism of documents, that man is Valla, even though he did not always follow up his insights. He suggested that the anonymous textbook of rhetoric commonly known as *ad Herennium* was not by Cicero; that the letters of St. Paul to Seneca were later fabrications; he voiced suspicions of 'pseudo-Isidore'; he was aware that 'pseudo-Dionysius' was not a contemporary of St. Paul, noting that Ambrose, Augustine and Jerome do not mention Dionysius, nor do Basil, St. Gregory Nazianzen and St. John Chrysostom. He was skilled at constructive criticism as well as destructive; his bold conjectures as to how the text of Livy should be emended (especially books 21-26) are famous. He applied similar methods to the text of the New Testament, in a book which was left unprinted till the next century, perhaps because it was thought too dangerous. For it must not be thought that Valla's contemporaries and the generations following accepted his doubts and arguments as valid; although so many of them have been virtually unchallenged since the seventeenth century, they were often criticised before. Agostino Steuco attacked Valla's attack on the Donation in his *Against L. Valla* (1546): and Robert Bellarmine called Valla a 'Lutheran' for his doubts about pseudo-Dionysius.[1] The way in which respect for the Bible as the word of God inhibited Valla's contemporaries may be seen from the fact that similar methods could quite easily be applied to the Koran in the fifteenth century. John of Segovia, who made a new translation of the Koran in the 1450s, suggested that the previous translator had introduced western ideas into the text. In 1460, Nicholas of Cusa wrote the *Sieving of the Koran* (Cribratio Alcoran) which treated the Koran as Nicholas had already treated the *Donation*. He identified three elements in its composition: Nestorian Christianity, a Jewish adviser of Muhammad, and the corruptions introduced by Jewish 'correctors' after Muhammad's death. This was to treat the Koran as a historical document, and to write the history of its leading ideas. It is difficult to say how far Valla was aware of the implications of what he was doing. His *Annotations on the New Testament* imply that he thought of the Bible as a historical document, written in particular historical circumstances, and, perhaps, simply one source among others. Was he aware of this implication? At any rate, the prologue to his biography of Ferdinand of Aragon, singing the praises of history, points out that historians came before philosophers: that

> Moses was a historian too, than whom there is no earlier and wiser writer; and the Evangelists (than whose works nothing is more judicious) ought to be called nothing other than 'historians'.

There is no one like Valla in the later fifteenth century; but Erasmus, who published Valla's *Annotations*, and was an admirer of his, carried on from where his predecessor left off. For example, he published an edition of the New Testament which went back behind the official Latin translation, the Vulgate, to the Greek. He demonstrated that the letter of Cyril to Augustine was not authentic. A favourite theme of Erasmus was that of 'return to the sources'.

---

[1] Luther did in fact argue, in his *Babylonish Captivity*, that Dionysius lived after the Fathers of the Church, not before them: Bellarmine might, with more historical sense, have called Luther a 'Vallan'.

C

If anyone wants to learn piety rather than disputation, let him straight away go to the sources (*versetur in fontibus*) and those writers who drank immediately from the sources.

> Erasmus, *Way of reaching true theology* (Ratio perveniendi ad veram theologiam), (1520) Basel, p. 217

In a similar spirit, John Colet, *c.* 1467-1519, a friend of Erasmus lectured on the New Testament at Oxord in the 1490s and compared it with other sources for ancient history; for example, he compares St. Paul's Epistle to the Romans with Suetonius's life of the emperor Claudius.

This Epistle to the Romans was written during the reign of Claudius, at the close of his reign, about the twentieth year of St. Paul's ministry. At which time also, as I gather from the histories and from the letters of St. Paul himself, both Epistles to the Corinthians were written, as well as that to the Galatians: but this one to the Romans after them, not long before St. Paul's last journey to Jerusalem. For he was imprisoned by Festus, the Governor of Judea, four or five years after the despatch of these letters, and sent by him to Rome. This was the twentyfifth year after the death of Christ, and after St. Paul's commission, and the second year of the reign of Nero. After this date he survived for twelve years and taught in Italy, and served under the banner of Christ till his death, – thirty-seven years from his first conversion. He perished in the first persecution of the Christians that continued under Nero, on the same day as St. Peter, in the fourteenth year of Nero's reign.

I mention this, that St. Paul's great thoughtfulness and prudence may be remarked. For being aware that Claudius Caesar had succeeded to the throne; a man of changeable disposition, and bad principles, and sudden purposes; a man too who, as Suetonius writes in his Life, banished the Jews from Rome, as they were in constant insurrection at the instigation of CHRESTUS (on account of which insurrection I suppose St. Paul to have written this Epistle, and that what Suetonius meant to convey was, that the Jews had been banished by Claudius on account of their disputes about Christ); – St. Paul understanding, I say, that the Roman Emperor, as Suetonius also relates, was levying some new and unheard of taxes, originated by Caligula, letting no description of persons or things escape without some amount of tribute being

imposed upon them; lest the brethren at Rome should chance to
become weary of their vexations and break forth into some con-
tumely and defiance of the Roman magistrates, and refuse to obey
their decrees; – St. Paul, I repeat, writing to those who professed
the service of Christ, to teach them something as to the behaviour
they were to show towards the Romans, and unbelieving rulers,
whose subjects they could not but be, if they lived at Rome, nor
avoid submitting to all their decrees, but must needs give them
somewhat, which was theirs, that they might keep on the other
hand what was their own, and render, as the Saviour commands,
unto Caesar the things that are Caesar's, and unto God the things
that are God's; – that most wise Apostle Paul, I repeat again,
perceiving that this must be done, exhorts and commands them
so to do, and on no account to contend with the Roman powers,
or give them any cause for being incensed and angry; but to maintain sincere charity among themselves, without variance, and to be
kind both towards one another and towards all else; that they
might stand firmly together in kindness, and by kindness, so far as
possible, ever prevail over their adversaries, and draw them to
goodness, and likeness to themselves, whilst they themselves were
on no account to be drawn to evil.

> J. Colet, *Exposition of St. Paul's Epistle to the
> Romans* ed. and trans. J. H. Lupton, (1873)
> London, pp. 94-6

A further stage in the rise of the view that the Bible is a historical
document is represented by William Perkins, a prominent Elizabethan
Calvinist theologian, who died in 1602. His view that the scripture
should be taken literally, and not, as it had been in the Middle Ages
(see Aquinas, above, p. 3) allegorically or tropologically, was a
common sixteenth-century Protestant view. By 1521, this was Luther's
opinion. Attacking the Louvain theologian Latomus, Luther criticised
'the Louvainian and Latomian way of separating the meaning of
Scripture from its context, consequences, and circumstances', and
argued that there should be no resort to figurative interpretations of the
Bible (above, p. 3) unless the context demanded it. Tyndale wrote
that 'the Scripture hath but one sense, which is the literal sense'. But
not all Protestants meant the same thing by 'literal', and Perkins' view
is more historical than most.

The Church of Rome maketh four senses of the Scriptures, the
literal, allegorical, tropological and anagogical ... but this her

device of the fourhold meaning of the Scripture must be exploded and rejected. There is one only sense, and the same is the literal . . . The supreme and absolute mean [measure] of interpretation is the Scripture itself . . . the means subordinated to the Scripture are three: the analogy of faith, the circumstances of the place propounded, and the comparing of places together . . . The circumstances of the place propounded are these: Who? to whom? upon what occasion? at what time? in what place? for what end? what goeth before? what followeth?

W. Perkins, *The Art of Prophesying*, in *Works*,
volume II, (1613) Cambridge, pp. 651-2

Perkins offers an example of Calvinist 'iconoclasm' in the field of textual criticism. It is not the only one. It was the Calvinist Isaac Casaubon, 1559-1614, who exposed some of the most famous forged, or rather misdated, texts; the works of 'Hermes Trismegistus'. In his method, Casaubon is in the tradition of Petrarch and Valla. In his conclusions, Casaubon shatters one of the most cherished Renaissance illusions; that of an ancient Egyptian wisdom miraculously foretelling platonic doctrines.

As for Hermes Trismegistus and the Sibylline Oracles which are also read today, it cannot be denied that they deal with many articles of religion, such as the one true God; the most holy Trinity; the Word, Son of God, by whom the world was created; the coming birth of Christ and the Virgin; Christ's passion and crucifixion; rebirth to eternal life by means of baptism; the Last Judgement; and so on. These matters are discussed so clearly that it is scarcely possible to find anything similar in the whole of the law of Moses and the Prophets. But I cannot hide my suspicions . . . I shall expound my reasons briefly here . . . I am moved above all by the argument that it seems contrary to the word of God for such deep mysteries to have been explained more clearly to the Gentiles than to that people whom God loved as His own, and instructed with his own voice and that of His faithful servants . . . For there is no doubt that Hermes Trismegistus lived before Moses, if anything that is said of him is certain . . . another argument which moves me is that in the writings of Plato, Aristotle, Theophrastus, and other pagans of wide learning, there is no trace of the things which we now see in Hermes or the Sibylline Books. Lastly, the following argument I find most forcible: that I see that in the days of the primitive Church there were many people who thought it a marvellous thing to add their own fantasies to divine truth, in order that the new doctrine might be accepted the more quickly by the wise men of the Gentiles. They called these lies white ones, invented for a worthy purpose ... But it is impossible not to condemn most severely what they did, and we marvel at the judgement of those Fathers of the Church who accepted writings of this kind so easily ... it was the work of Time to bring this deception to light ...

(Casaubon proceeds to examine the ideas and the style of 'Pseudomercurius' in more detail.)

We declare that this book contains not the Egyptian doctrine of Hermes, but a mixture of Greek and Christian ideas taken partly from the works of Plato and the Platonists, sometimes using their very own words, and partly from the Bible ... I come to the style, and the stories which this writer mentions in passing. Since it is agreed that Hermes the Egyptian lived in the earliest times, about the year 200 from the creation of the world, this book cannot have been written by him, because it mentions the sculptures of Phidias ... Then again, if this book were really by Hermes, it would be necessary either for him to have written it himself in Greek, or for someone else to have translated it from Egyptian. But we deny both possibilities: the first, because the style of this book is quite different from that of the Greeks who were the contemporaries of Hermes; for that old language contained many words and many phrases, in fact the whole structure of it was quite different from that used by the later Greeks ... I also deny that it was translated from another language ... for no translation was ever made, so well that it did not reveal its foreignness by certain qualities.

I. Casaubon, *On Sacred Matters*, (1614) London, pp. 71-86

Two younger men, both Calvinist ministers, produced the definitive exposures of two more celebrated forgeries. David Blondel, 1590-1655, exposed the false decretals in his *Pseudo-Isidorus* (1628) and Jean Daillé, 1549-1670, exposed Pseudo-Dionysius (together with some writings attributed to Ignatius of Antioch) in a book published in 1666. Valla's suspicions had thus been turned into full demonstrations in the manner of his criticisms of the Donation of Constantine. At much the same time, belief in the pseudo-historians of the Trojan War, Dictys the

Cretan and Dares the Phrygian, was finally abandoned. It was J. J. Scaliger, the chronologist (above, p. 47) who voiced the most celebrated doubts of their authenticity in a letter to Casaubon of 1605.

It may well occasion surprise that Valla's insights should have taken so long to be followed up. The reason is surely the destructive implications of these exposures of myth for traditional religious beliefs; too much of pseudo-Dionysius and pseudo-Isidore had become incorporated in Catholicism for their disappearance to be accepted lightly. For Calvinists, these particular discoveries were less of an embarrassment. In the case of the historical interpretation of the Bible, however, (textual emendations, revised ascriptions of authorship, and so on), the implications of research were destructive for the new orthodoxies of Luther and Calvin as well as for traditional Catholicism, and scholars were still more wary of following in the footsteps of Valla. A common attitude was expressed by Sir Thomas Browne in his *Religio Medici*:

> ... it is not a warrantable curiosity to examine the verity of Scripture by the concordance of human history, or seek to confirm the chronology of Hester or Daniel by the authority of Megasthenes or Herodotus.
>
> T. Browne, *Religio Medici*, written *c.* 1635,
> first pub. 1642, (1906), London, p. 34

Fortunately for the discipline of history, some people in the sixteenth and seventeenth centuries did think this kind of curiosity warrantable. Luther's radical contemporary Andreas von Karlstadt declared in 1520 that Moses was not the author of the Pentateuch.[1] The great scholar Scaliger declared the letter of Aristeas to Philocrates (a letter which was used to support the Septuagint)[2] to be a forgery. Archbishop Ussher, unlike his contemporary Thomas Browne, believed in trying to make a concordance of Biblical and secular chronology. In the mid seventeenth-century, Karlstadt's problem was taken up again: Isaac de la Peyrere, a Calvinist of Bordeaux, argued in 1655 that Moses did not write the Pentateuch. He was imprisoned. The same point was made a few years later by Baruch Spinoza, 1623-77, in his *Theologico-Political Treatise*. The book was published anonymously, and even the printer used a pseudonym; this in the Dutch Republic, the home of religious toleration. The *Treatise* was in fact prohibited by the Dutch States-General four years later. Shortly afterwards, the French Oratorian, Richard Simon, made the same point – that Moses could not have

---

[1] The first five books of the Old Testament.
[2] The earliest Greek translation of the Old Testament.

been the author of all the books traditionally attributed to him – in his *Critical History of the Old Testament* (1678). Bossuet, who might be described as Louis XIV's official theologian, saw this passage, declared that Simon wanted to sap the foundations of religion, and had the book suppressed. Simon was also expelled from his order.

Of all these Biblical critics, Spinoza is the most interesting in the context of this chapter, because he goes furthest towards regarding the Bible as a historical document. He is in the tradition of Valla and Erasmus, and the Enlightenment follows on from him.

The method of interpreting Scripture does not widely differ from the method of interpreting nature – in fact, it is almost the same. For as the interpretation of nature consists in the examination of the history of nature, and therefrom deducing definitions of natural phenomena on certain fixed axioms, so Scriptural interpretation proceeds by the examination of Scripture, and inferring the intention of its authors as a legitimate conclusion from its fundamental principles. By working in this manner everyone will always advance without danger of error – that is, if they admit no principles for interpreting Scripture, and discussing its contents save such as they find in Scripture itself – and will be able with equal security to discuss what surpasses our understanding, and what is known by the natural light of reason . . .

The universal rule, then, in interpreting Scripture is to accept nothing as an authoritative Scriptural statement which we do not perceive very clearly when we examine it in the light of its history. What I mean by its history, and what should be the chief points elucidated, I will now explain.

The history of a Scriptural statement comprises:

I. The nature and properties of the language in which the books of the Bible were written, and in which their authors were accustomed to speak. We shall thus be able to investigate every expression by comparison with common conversational usages. . . .

II. An analysis of each book and arrangement of its contents under heads; so that we may have at hand the various texts which treat of a given subject. Lastly, a note of all the passages which are ambiguous or obscure, or which seem mutually contradictory.

I call passages clear or obscure according as their meaning is inferred easily or with difficulty in relation to the context, not according as their truth is perceived easily or the reverse by reason. We are at work not on the truth of passages, but solely on their meaning. We must take especial care, when we are in search of the meaning of a text, not to be led away by our reason in so far as it is founded on principles of natural knowledge (to say nothing of prejudices): in order not to confound the meaning of a passage with its truth, we must examine it solely by means of the signification of the words, or by a reason acknowledging no foundation but Scripture.

I will illustrate my meaning by an example. The words of Moses, 'God is a fire' and 'God is jealous', are perfectly clear so long as we regard merely the signification of the words, and I therefore reckon them among the clear passages, though in relation to reason and truth they are most obscure: still, although the literal meaning is repugnant to the natural light of reason, nevertheless, if it cannot be clearly overruled on grounds and principles derived from its Scriptural 'history', it, that is the literal meaning, must be the one retained: and contrariwise if these passages literally interpreted are found to clash with principles derived from Scripture, though such literal interpretation were in absolute harmony with reason, they must be understood in a different manner, i.e. metaphorically.

If we would know whether Moses believed God to be a fire or not, we must on no account decide the question on grounds of the reasonableness or the reverse of such an opinion, but must judge solely by the other opinions of Moses which are on record.

In the present instance, as Moses says in several other passages that God has no likeness to any visible thing, whether in heaven or in earth, or in the water, either all such passages are to be taken metaphorically, or else the one before us must be so explained. However, as we should depart as little as possible from the literal sense, we must first ask whether this text, God is a fire, admits of any but the literal meaning – that is, whether the word fire ever means anything besides ordinary natural fire . . . as we find the name fire applied to anger and jealousy (see Job xxxi.12) we can thus easily reconcile the words of Moses, and legitimately conclude that the two propositions God is a fire, and God is jealous, are in meaning identical.

Further, as Moses clearly teaches that God is jealous, and nowhere states that God is without passions or emotions, we must evidently infer that Moses held this doctrine himself, or at any rate, that he wished to teach it, nor must we refrain because such a belief seems contrary to reason: for as we have shown, we cannot wrest the meaning of texts to suit the dictates of our reason, or our preconceived opinions. The whole knowledge of the Bible must be sought solely from itself.

III. Lastly, such a history should relate the environment of all the prophetic books extant; that is, the life, the conduct, and the studies of the author of each book, who he was, what was the occasion and the epoch of his writing, whom did he write for, and in what language. Further, it should inquire into the fate of each book: how it was first received, into whose hands it fell, how many different versions there were of it, by whose advice was it received into the Bible, and, lastly, how all the books now universally accepted as sacred, were united into a single whole.

All such information should, as I have said, be contained in the 'history' of scripture. For, in order to know what statements are set forth as laws, and what as moral precepts, it is important to be acquainted with the life, the conduct, and the pursuits of their author: moreover, it becomes easier to explain a man's writings in proportion as we have more intimate knowledge of his genius and temperament.

Furthermore, that we may not confound precepts which are eternal with those which served only a temporary purpose, or were only meant for a few, we should know what was the occasion, the time, the age, in which each book was written, and to what nation it was addressed.

> Benedict Spinoza, *Tractatus Theologico-Politicus*,
> (1670), trans. R. H. M. Elwes, (1891) London

This was (as contemporaries pointed out) to bring the Bible down to the level of the works of Homer and Aristotle.

It was also in the seventeenth century that the new critical approach to sources was turned into a system. The Benedictine Jean Mabillon, 1632-1707, wrote a book *On Diplomatic* (1681) which created a new subject, 'diplomatic': the science, or art, of dating documents, and recognising forged ones, on the basis of their form.

This chapter has so far been largely concerned with examples from Church history, or the history of theology. This is in fact the area where most advances were made, most falsifications detected. However, secular examples are also to be found, besides Petrarch's exposure of the Austrian privilege. In England, John Selden, 1584-1654 showed that the *Manner of Holding Parliament* (*Modus Tenendi Parliamentum*) did not date from the time of William the Conqueror, as was commonly believed, but from the fourteenth century,

> trust not to its pretended antiquity – it cannot be of the Conqueror's age. Many men have copies of it, but none hath ever been seen very ancient.
>
> J. Selden, *Titles of Honour*, (1614) London, p. 274

Another example of Selden at work, which shows his patient construction of a proof, is his dating of the legal commentary known as the 'Fleta'.

> From the preface it is clear that the treatise was written under one of the Edwards, but whether First, Second or Third is not indicated, the reference being to 'Edward our King' . . . Did he write under Edward III? In my opinion No, because he cites statutes of Edward I on shipwreck, dower and other things and frequently quotes laws of Henry III, whereas he mentions no statute of Edward III's reign. This would not have been so had he lived in the reign of the third Edward . . . Similarly, it may be argued that he did not write it later than the year 1320, since, in his exhaustive treatment of Convictions, he makes no mention of the Act passed 13 Edward II which concerns Attaints, nor does he at any time quote from any of the acts of Edward II's day. In the absence of contrary proof, therefore, it may be assumed that he wrote before Edward II's reign . . . Elsewhere in the treatise there are clear indications that it was written in Edward I's reign. Thus in speaking of the privileges of the Templars he refers to them, equally with the Knights Hospitallers, as flourishing in his time, whereas only those quite ignorant of our law and history are unaware of the fact that by Edward II's reign the Templars had completely disappeared from England. Secondly, in defining the writ *Moderata Misericordia*, based on a clause in Magna Carta, he frames the words to suit his time, speaking in the royal name of 'the import of Magna Carta of King Henry our Father . . .', obviously Henry III, father of Edward I. Thirdly, he writes 'Our Lord the King lately in his parliament of Acton Burnell'. This parliament was held 11 Edward I and the words 'Our Lord the King' were commonly used of the reigning monarch. Fourthly, he explicitly refers to statutes passed in the 13th year of the king's reign – by this Edward I's 'Statute of Merchants' is obviously

meant. Lastly, he speaks of Henry II as the great-grandfather of
the king under whom he wrote and everyone knows that Edward
I was the great-grandson of Henry II.

> John Selden, *Dissertation on the Fleta*, (1647), ed.
> and trans. David Ogg, (1925) Cambridge,
> 177-85

Two prefaces by Selden sum up the new attitude towards sources.
In the first, he declares,

> Wherever my inquisition might aid, I vent to you nothing quoted
> at second hand, but ever loved the fountain, and, when I could
> come at it, used that medium only, which would not at all, or
> least, deceive by refraction.

> J. Selden, *Titles of Honour*, (1614) London

In the second, he makes a conscious parallel between philosophical and
historical scepticism.

> The old sceptics that would never profess that they had found a
> truth, showed yet the best way to search for any . . . he that
> avoids their disputing levity yet . . . takes to himself their liberty
> of enquiry, is in the only way that in all kinds of studies leads and
> lies open even to the sanctuary of truth.

> J. Selden, *History of Tithes*, (1617) London

Renaissance historical scepticism was extended to evidence which
was not literary. Two sixteenth-century treatises, Enea Vico's *Discourses
on Ancient Medals* (Venice, 1555) and Antonio Agustín's *Dialogues on
Medals* (Tarragona, 1587) discuss how forged medals and coins can be
detected.

## 2   The Criticism of Myths

The criticism of documents and the criticism of myths are obviously
connected; what Valla was arguing, for example, was that the story of
Constantine's gift to Sylvester was not fact but myth, supporting his
claim by denouncing the document of 'donation' as a forgery. Again,
Valla was prepared to argue (unlike Dante) that Livy had made mistakes – about the genealogy of the Tarquins, for example. In the
sixteenth and seventeenth centuries, a number of famous myths were
exploded. Erasmus began the critical approach to the lives of the saints
with the short biography which he wrote as a preface to his edition of
Jerome's works; he tried to go back to the sources, and to write the

life of Jerome 'as it actually happened'. As Erasmus put it himself,

> I think nothing more right than to describe the saints just as
> they were; if it is discovered that they made mistakes, this too will
> be a good example for us. If anyone really wants inventions, let
> him prudently create an image of a pious man, whatever his name,
> who knows and follows Christ's own teaching and has the inner
> force of the piety of the early Church; I can perhaps tolerate that.
> But let us do without sackcloth, hair-shirts, whips, prodigious
> fasts, and unbelievable vigils. All the same, let a craftsman imitate
> the light and splendour of any jewel; the copy will never match
> the power of the original jewel. Truth too has its power, and can-
> not be matched by any imitation. Who can tolerate the people
> who do not celebrate but rather contaminate the saints with their
> old wives' tales, which are childish, ignorant, and absurd? . . .
>
> There were no secondary works (*commentarii*) which could be
> trusted, so in good faith and with diligence we did research on the
> life of this holy man in Prosperus, Severus, Orosius, Ruffinus
> (although he is a detractor) and other authors who are not to be
> distrusted completely; however, we relied most of all on the
> works of Jerome himself. For who knew Jerome better than
> Jerome himself? Who expressed his ideas more faithfully? If
> Julius Caesar is the most reliable source for the events of his own
> career, is it not all the more reasonable to trust Jerome on his? And
> so, having gone through all his books, we made a few annotations
> and presented the results in the form of a narrative, not concealing
> the fact that we consider it a great enough miracle to have Jerome
> himself explaining his life to us in all his famous books. If there is
> anyone who must have his miracles and omens, let him read the
> books about Jerome which contain almost as many miracles as
> they do sentences.

Trans. from Erasmi Opuscula, ed. W. K.<br>Ferguson, (1933) The Hague, pp. 136-9

Naturally, St. Jerome's lion (above, p. 9) had to disappear. In the
seventeenth century this new approach to the lives of the saints became
more definite and systematic. Of great importance in this process were
a group of Jesuit scholars known as the Bollandists after one of them,
Jean Bolland, 1596-1655; also important were Heribert Roswey,
1569-1629, whose edition of the *Lives of the Fathers* may be said to
mark the beginning of their enterprise, and Godefroid Henskens, 1601-
81. Their task was to rewrite the lives of all the saints in the calendar

on the basis of original sources – a herculean task, in the course of which many cherished beliefs turned out to be without foundation. One Bollandist, Papebroch, had a bitter controversy with the Carmelite provincial, after he had denied that the Carmelite order had been founded by the prophet Elijah.

The problem was, as Robert Bellarmine frankly confined to Roswey, that the original sources for the lives of the saints abounded in improbabilities and stories which could not be taken seriously, and that if all the saints were removed from the martyrology who should be removed, there would hardly be any martyrology left.

It was not only religious myths that came under attack; there were secular ones too, particularly the stories of the origin of nations, France and England for example, which no longer commanded belief.

The Scottish historian, John Major, 1469-1550, in his *History of Great Britain* (1521) had little time for the story of Brutus and the foundation of Britain as retailed by Geoffrey of Monmouth and his successors (above, p. 8). He also dismissed the story of Scota, Pharaoh's daughter, giving her name to Scotland. Still more devastating were the criticisms made of Brutus by the Italian historian, Polydore Vergil, in his *History of England* published in 1534. Discussing Geoffrey of Monmouth, Polydore writes as follows.

It is mentioned in that book . . . that Brutus the son of Sylvius, who (as is well known) was begotten of Ascanius the son of Aeneas, after his passage through Greece, and conquest of Aquitaine, arrived at Britain, according to the admonition of the goddess Diana; where at his first entry, vanquishing those giants which at that time possessed the island and ran to repel the force of foreigners, did himself occupy the country, calling it according to his own name Britain; and so to conclude that Brutus was the author of the British nation, who, begetting sons, enhanced them and enlarged his dominion wondrously. But yet neither Livy, neither Dionysius Halicarnasseus, who wrote diligently of the Roman antiquities, nor divers other writers, did ever once make rehearsal of this Brutus, neither could that be notified [established] by the chronicles of the Britons, since that long ago they lost all the books of their monuments, as Gildas witnesseth, who flourished about the 580th year of our salvation . . . But in old time they did presume on this franchise and liberty that many nations were so bold as to derive the beginning of their stock from the Gods (as especially the Romans did), to the entent the original of their people and cities might be more princely and prosperous, which things, albeit they sounded more like fables than the sincere witnesses of noble acts, yet were they received for truth; for the which cause even those things which last of all were committed to writing of the antiquities of Britain, were with so easy credit received of the common sort that they have ascribed the fountain of their genealogy to Brutus . . .

Now as touching myself, albeit I have steadfastly promised that I will neither affirm as true, neither reprove as false, the judgment of one or other as concerning the original of so ancient a people, referring all things, as we have done heretofore, to the consideration of the reader; nevertheless after the matter shall be committed to conjecture, I shall utter in this place that which shall not altogether seem abhorrent from truth . . . seeing the island, on bright days, may easily be seen from the French shore, and hath a far off given prospect unto the sailors by reason of the white rocks about the bank (whereof it was called Albion), surely it could never be obscure or unknown to the regions lying around it. Wherefore it is not to be thought that at any time it lacked inhabitants . . .

But whither shall we go, seeing that all things are full of darkness. Truly there is nothing more obscure, more uncertain, or unknown than the affairs of the Britons from the beginning; partly because the chronicles, if there were any, were clean destroyed (as we said before), according to the testimonial of Gildas; partly because the nation, as it is placed far from all others, so was it long unknown to the Romans and Grecians. This silence was the cause why good authors have not left in memory very many things of the original of these countrymen; and many on the other side have been bold to speak so largely, and to make such a strange history thereof, that in the admiration of the common people (who always more regard novelties than truth) they seem to be in heaven, where with a good will I will leave them, thinking it not good to debate the matter with them as touching these feigned trifles.

> P. Vergil, *History of England*, (1543), ed. Sir
> Henry Ellis, (1846) London, pp. 30-33;
> spelling modernised

Polydore's exposure of myth was coupled with the exposure of a forgery, for he edited Gildas's book and argued that the 'Commentary of Gildas' was not by Gildas at all. All the same, in the sixteenth century, most British scholars were on the side of Geoffrey against

Polydore; Camden being an important exception. It was only in the seventeenth century – a crucial century in the history of scepticism – that the balance swung the other way.

Similarly, in sixteenth-century France, scholars began to have doubts about the Trojan origin of the Gauls and about the existence of Francion, eponymous founder of France as Brutus was of Britain – Étienne Pasquier, for example.

> As for the Trojans, it is truly extraordinary how every nation agrees to feel greatly honoured to take its ancient stock from the destruction of Troy. In this way the Romans claim that their founder was Aeneas: the French, Francion: the Turks, Turcus: the British, Brutus: and the first inhabitants of the Adriatic boasted of an Antenor [c.f. Biondo on the foundation of Padua, above, p. 29.] It is as if Troy had been a nursery of knights, who were responsible for the origin of all other countries, and as if divine providence had caused the ruin of one nation to bring about the rise to fame of a hundred others. For my part, I dare neither to contradict this opinion nor to assent to it. It seems to me that it is a very delicate matter to dispute about the origin of nations. For in the beginning, they were so small that ancient writers did not bother to spend their time discussing their origins, so that little by little the memory of those origins completely disappeared, or was changed into beautiful but implausible myths. A similar mistake is made by those who vainly labour to tell us from the surviving evidence and the etymology who was the founder of each town. Not that I wish to assert that this is never possible; but it is only possible when a prince or great lord has deliberately undertaken to build one or make it independent, with unusual magnificence. Thus Constantinople was founded by Constantine, and Alexandria in Egypt by Alexander the Great. Yet there are so many towns which in the course of time, perhaps because the climate is temperate, perhaps because of their suitability to trade, or because princes take delight in them, have become so great that they have supplanted many others; but whoever wished to find out who laid the first stone of them, would find his difficulty as great as those of our annalists, who simply had recourse to the Trojans.
>
> E. Pasquier, *Researches on France*, book 1, (1560)
> Paris, chapter 14

Again, Gabriel Naudé, 1600-1653, attacked the 'fable' of Francion and national myths in general.

For there is scarcely a nation which does not flatter itself about its origins, and take its beginning back to some hero or demigod; our Frenchmen have been so jealous of this honour that they have looked in fables for what they could not obtain from facts.

> G. Naudé, *Addition to the History of Louis XI*,
> (1630) Paris, p. 25

As in England, the new opinions took time to succeed. A few years after Pasquier, Ronsard published his *Franciade* (1572) a sort of French *Aeneid* written round that very Francion whom Pasquier had been trying to undermine. In the mid-seventeenth century, Mézeray still began his *History of France* with the equally mythical Pharamond.

Another example of Pasquier's criticism of venerable myths is his discussion of the claim of the university of Paris to have been founded by Charlemagne.

It is no small honour to this noble university, if it has for godfather the emperor Charlemagne, who has been given such a title, just as I see that he is credited with the foundation of our parlements and of the twelve peers of France ... he was a truly great prince ... but for my part I do not believe that either the parlements or the peers were founded by him, as I have shown in detail in book II, nor do I believe that he founded the university of Paris ... do not think that it is out of desire for novelty or contradiction that I take up this new opinion. I know what respect is owed to a generally received opinion, but I also know that I owe still greater respect to the truth. So I will say again that Charlemagne would have been no mean founder of our University; all the same, I find no mention of this foundation in Aimoin, Rheginon, Adon or Sigisbert. As for Turpin's history, it is not authentic and it does not mention this either. Yet it is a matter which they would not have passed over in silence, but mentioned to our great honour, since they stopped to mention many lesser events. Einhard who says he had been Charlemagne's secretary, seems to have left the emperor's military exploits to other historians, and taken the emperor's culture as his own share, telling us that Charlemagne was brought up to know several foreign languages as well as his own, and more particularly that Latin was as familiar to him as his mother tongue. As for Greek, he understood it, although he could not pronounce it ... In short, since Einhard's main point about Charlemagne was his devotion to literature and other sorts of knowledge, I cannot persuade myself that he would not have

ended by mentioning the university if Charlemagne had been its
founder, as much because of the dignity of the place where it had
been established (the ancient seat of the Kings of France from the
time of Clovis), as for the excellence of the foundation itself.

> E. Pasquier, *Researches on France*, book 9, (1665
> edition) Paris, chapter 5, p. 766

Although Pasquier would not deny that Dionysius-Denis founded
the French Church, he clearly did not think he did. This story was, he
said, 'an article of history, not of faith': it could be rejected.

Again, there is an English parallel; in the sixteenth century, Oxford
men believed that their university had been founded by King Alfred,
Cambridge men that theirs went back to King Arthur or before.

But Sir Simons D'Ewes remarked in Parliament in 1641,

> If I should lose time to reckon up the vain allegations produced for
> the antiquity of Oxford by Twyne, and of Cambridge by Caius,
> I should but repeat *deliria senum* [senilities]: for I account the most
> of that they have published in print to be no better.

> Cited in James Parker, *The Early History of
> Oxford*, (1885) Oxford, p. 12

More generalised forms of scepticism are rare in the Renaissance,
Agrippa von Nettesheim devoted a chapter to the vanity of writing
history in his book on the uncertainty and vanity of all subjects, but
this is not much more than a rhetorical exercise, though in passing he
does make a valid and damaging criticism of the extent to which the
histories written in his day were vitiated by the desire to flatter patrons.
Sir Philip Sidney's attack on history in his defence of poetry has again
a great deal of the rhetorical exercise about it, though he too introduces
criticisms which ring true and are not often made in the period, like
his description of the historian as 'authorising himself for the most
part upon other histories, whose greatest authorities are built upon the
notable foundations of hearsay'. For more serious doubts one has to
wait till the seventeenth century, when Descartes suggested that history
was as dangerous a guide to life as romances of chivalry, because
historians always left out significant details, thinking them beneath the
dignity of history; and La Mothe le Vayer wrote a book entitled *On
how little Certainty there is in History* (published 1668).

Of course, not all Renaissance historians were critical in their use of
sources: not everyone exposed myths. Many people believed in myths
like those of Brutus and Francion, professional scholars included. Some

myths may well have been invented during the Renaissance; for example, the myths of the royal oath and the ancient laws of the Aragonese (including the right of resistance) seem to go back to the 1560s only, and their function is clear: to justify the privileges of the Aragonese against encroachments of royal power. Much narrative history was still composed by a kind of 'bricolage', by paraphrasing and incorporating in a narrative passages from previous narratives, which were treated as 'authorities' without an attempt being made to return to their sources.

Given these qualifications, which are serious ones, I think that it is still possible to argue that the Renaissance was a time when historians developed a new awareness of evidence. It can be seen most spectacularly in the criticism of documents and the criticism of myths, but it is noticeable in other ways too. Some sixteenth-century historians, like Guicciardini, Sleidan, and Camden, made good use of documents when writing their narratives; Sleidan, for example, worked in the archives of Philip of Hesse and in those of Strasbourg. Camden described his achievement to the reader not unfairly when he wrote, 'I have been diligent in the records of his realm . . . I have pored upon many an old roll and evidence.' During the sixteenth and seventeenth centuries, one can find the publication of documents used as a new weapon of controversy. For example, Gallican critics of the Council of Trent used this method: in 1607 Jacques Gillot published the *Acts of the Council of Trent*, and in 1608, letters of French kings and French ambassadors to the Council. In the controversy about the blame for the outbreak of the Thirty Years' War (if the convenient anachronism be pardoned) in the 1620s, documents were taken seriously. After the battle of the White Mountain, the documents of the Anhalt chancery were captured by the imperial forces, and a pamphlet was published in 1621 which made use of them and was called 'the Anhalt chancery'; but then Mansfield's soldiers captured an imperial courier, and the other side was able to bring out 'the Spanish chancery' in the following year.

The new awareness of evidence is one of the greatest intellectual achievements of Renaissance Europe. It is the real 'historical revolution' comparable to the scientific revolution. All the same, it must be added that what was developed was a sense of the importance of primary sources, and a capacity for detecting sources which were not primary, although they claimed to be. It was not until the eighteenth and nineteenth centuries that western historians developed the art of doubting what is in primary sources, and of extracting from them information that their authors would not have known that they possessed.

# IV

# HISTORICAL EXPLANATION

## 1 The Rise of Explanation

In the first chapter, I suggested that in medieval historical writing there are explanations of an extremely specific kind, in terms of the motives of individuals; there are also explanations of an extremely general kind, in terms of the hand of God in history, or the decay of the world; but middle-range explanations are lacking. Since the eighteenth century, it is just these middle-range explanations, whether given in terms of the social structure or the climate of opinion, the spirit of the age or the state of the economy, which have interested historians most. In the sixteenth century, there is a move towards this type of explanation. 'Fortune', that favourite medieval and Renaissance concept, becomes less and less anthropomorphised, less and less the goddess one must grasp by the forelock, and more of a name for the impersonal forces in history, the structures and the trends which are bigger than individuals, but which are susceptible of analysis and calculation all the same. Such a view of fortune emerges clearly from the twenty-fifth chapter of Machiavelli's *Prince*, written between 1513 and 1514, entitled 'how far human affairs are governed by fortune, and how fortune can be opposed'. Note especially his analysis of the policy of pope Julius II, who had the luck to live at a time when his impetuous temperament harmonised with external political circumstances, the *qualità de'tempi*, as Machiavelli calls it.

> I am not unaware that many have held and hold the opinion that events are controlled by fortune and by God in such a way that the prudence of men cannot modify them, indeed, that men have no influence whatsoever. Because of this, they would conclude that there is no point in sweating over things, but that one should submit to the rulings of chance. This opinion has been more widely held in our own times, because of the great changes and variations, beyond human imagining, which we have experienced

and experience every day. Sometimes, when thinking of this, I have myself inclined to this same opinion. Nonetheless, because free choice cannot be ruled out, I believe that it is probably true that fortune is the arbiter of half the things we do, leaving the other half or so to be controlled by ourselves. I compare fortune to one of those violent rivers which, when they are enraged, flood the plains, tear down trees and buildings, wash soil from one place to deposit it in another. Everyone flees before them, everybody yields to their impetus, there is no possibility of resistance. Yet although such is their nature, it does not follow that when they are flowing quietly one cannot take precautions, constructing dykes and embankments so that when the river is in flood it runs into a canal or else its impetus is less wild and dangerous. So it is with fortune. She shows her power where there is no force to hold her in check; and her impetus is felt where she knows there are no embankments and dykes built to restrain her. If you consider Italy, the theatre of those changes and variations I mentioned, which first appeared here, you will see that she is a country without embankments and without dykes: for if Italy had been adequately reinforced, like Germany, Spain, and France, either this flood would not have caused the great changes it has, or it would not have swept in at all.

I want what I have said to suffice, in general terms, on the question of how to oppose fortune. But, confining myself now to particular circumstances, I say that we see that some princes flourish one day and come to grief the next, without appearing to have changed in character or any other way. This I believe arises, first, for the reasons discussed at length earlier on, that is, that those princes who are utterly dependent on fortune come to grief when their fortune changes. I also believe that the one who adapts his policy to the times prospers, and likewise that the one whose policy clashes with the demands of the times does not. It can be observed that men use various methods in pursuing their own personal objectives, namely, glory and riches. One man proceeds with circumspection, another impetuously; one uses violence, another stratagem; one man goes about things patiently, another does the opposite; and yet everyone, for all this diversity of method, can reach his objective. It can also be observed that with two circumspect men, one will achieve his end, the other not; and likewise two men succeed equally well with different methods, one of them being circumspect and the other impetuous. This results from nothing else except the extent to which their methods are or are not suited to the nature of the times. Thus it happens that, as I have said, two men, working in different ways, can achieve the same end, and of two men working in the same way one gets what he wants and the other does not. This also explains why prosperity is ephemeral; because if a man behaves with patience and circumspection and the time and circumstances are such that this method is called for, he will prosper; but if time and circumstances change he will be ruined because he does not change his policy. Nor do we find any man shrewd enough to know how to adapt his policy in this way; either because he cannot do otherwise than what is in character or because, having always prospered by proceeding one way, he cannot persuade himself to change. Thus a man who is circumspect, when circumstances demand impetuous behaviour, is unequal to the task, and so he comes to grief. If he changed his character according to the time and circumstances, then his fortune would not change.

Pope Julius II was impetuous in everything; and he found the time and circumstances so favourable to his way of proceeding that he always met with success. Consider his first campaign, against Bologna, when messer Giovanni Bentivogli was still living. The Venetians mistrusted it; so did the king of Spain; and Julius was still arguing about the enterprise with France. Nonetheless, with typical forcefulness and impetuosity, he launched the expedition in person. This move disconcerted and arrested Spain and the Venetians, the latter because they were afraid and the former because of the king's ambition to reconquer all the kingdom of Naples. On the other hand, he drew the king of France after him. This was because the king, seeing Julius go into action, and anxious for his support in subduing the Venetians, decided he could not refuse him troops without doing him a manifest disservice. With that impetuous move of his, therefore, Julius achieved what no other pontiff, with the utmost human prudence, would have achieved. Because had Julius delayed setting out from Rome until all his plans and negotiations were completed, as any other pontiff would have done, he would never have succeeded. The king of France would have found a hundred and one excuses, and the others given him a hundred and one reasons for being afraid. I shall not discuss his other deeds, which were all like this and which all met with success. The brevity of his pontifical life did not let him experience the contrary. If there had come a time when it was necessary for him to act with circumspection he would have come to grief: he would never have acted other than in character.

I conclude, therefore, that as fortune is changeable while men are obstinate in their ways, men prosper so long as fortune and policy are in accord, and when there is a clash they fail. I hold strongly to this: that it is better to be impetuous than circumspect; because fortune is a woman and if she is to be submissive it is necessary to beat and coerce her. Experience shows that she is more often subdued by men who do this than by those who act coldly. Always, being a woman, she favours young men, because they are less circumspect and more ardent, and because they command her with greater audacity.

> N. Machiavelli, *The Prince*, (c. 1514), trans.
> G. Bull, (1961), pp. 130

Another example of Machiavelli's historical explanation, from his *History of Florence* this time, makes an interesting contrast with the passage from Villani quoted in chapter 1 (above, p. 16) because of its different approach to the same events. Where Villani's explanations were religious and moral, Machiavelli's are secular; again, Machiavelli does not stand alone but exemplifies a general change in European thought. In this case, Machiavelli analyses events in terms of individual motives, though he does go on to make a more general point about the nature of the Florentines a few pages later, suggesting that it is natural to them to find every administration distasteful, and for any occurrence to divide them.

> Our city was never greater or more prosperous than at this time, since it was full of men, riches and honour. There were 30 000 citizens who could bear arms in the city, and 70 000 in the country round. The whole of Tuscany obeyed Florence, because they were either friends or subjects of the Florentines. Although the nobles and the people were somewhat hostile and suspicious of one another, no ill results followed, and they lived in peace and unity. If this peace had not been disturbed by more internal conflicts, there would have been nothing to fear from outside, because the city was in such a state as not to fear the empire and her exiles any longer, and strong enough to defend herself against all the states of Italy. However, the harm that outsiders were unable to do Florence, was brought about by those within.
>
> There were in Florence two families who were extremely rich,

noble, and powerful, the Cerchi and the Donati. They were neighbours in Florence and in the countryside, and so there was some ill feeling between them, but not so serious for them to have recourse to arms. These evil humours would, perhaps, have had no great consequences, had they not been made worse by something new . . . [Machiavelli now tells the story of the split between the members of the Cancellieri family in Pistoia, and the consequent division of the city into Whites and Blacks. (See above, p. 16). Machiavelli goes on to describe the career of Corso Donati, head of the Donati.]

After the departure of Charles [of Anjou] life in Florence was quiet. Only messer Corso was restless, because he did not hold the rank in the city to which he felt himself entitled. The administration was one of the popolari, and so he saw the republic run by men inferior to himself in status. These were his real motives, but he thought to disguise his dishonourable intentions with an honourable pretext. So he accused many citizens who had had charge of public money of using it for their private benefit; and he declared that it would be good to find them out and punish them. He was supported by many who had the same intentions as himself, and by many others out of ignorance, since they thought that messer Corso was motivated by patriotism. On the other hand the citizens he had accused, who had popular support, defended themselves; and this disagreement went so far that after civil means, they had recourse to arms.

N. Machiavelli, *Florentine Histories*, (1532)
Rome, book II, chapters 15, 16, 21

Another classic example of historical analysis comes from the *History of Italy* written by Machiavelli's younger contemporary, Francesco Guicciardini, 1483-1540. His problem is to account for the disastrous foreign invasions which Italy suffered from the year 1492 onwards, and he does this partly in terms of the abilities and motives of individuals, partly in more structural terms, for example the balance of power, always emphasising (as Machiavelli often does not) the multiplicity and diversity of causes, and the conjectural element in explanations. He suggests that the calamities of Italy began when the whole country was enjoying a golden age of peace and prosperity.

Italy was preserved in this happy state, which had been attained through a variety of causes, by a number of circumstances, but among these by common consent no little credit was due to the industry and virtue of Lorenzo de'Medici, a citizen so far above the rank of private citizen in Florence that all the affairs of the Republic were decided by his advice. Florence was at that time powerful by virtue of her geographical position, the intelligence of her people and the readiness of her wealth rather than for the extent of her dominion. Lorenzo had lately allied himself through marriage to Pope Innocent VIII (who listened readily to his counsels); his name was respected throughout Italy and his authority was great in all discussions on matters of common interest. Knowing that it would be very dangerous to himself and to the Florentine Republic if any of the larger states increased their power, he diligently sought to maintain the affairs of Italy in such a balance that they might not favour one side more than another. This would not have been possible without the preservation of peace and without the most careful watch over any disturbance, however small. Ferdinand of Aragon, King of Naples, shared his desire for universal peace, undoubtedly a most prudent and respected prince; though in the past he had often shown ambitious designs contrary to the counsels of peace . . . Perhaps because a few years earlier he had experienced, with the gravest danger, the hatred of his barons and of his common subjects, and knowing the affection which many of his people still hold for the name of the royal house of France, he was afraid that discord in Italy might give the French an opportunity to attack the Kingdom of Naples. Or perhaps he realised that to balance the power of the Venetians, which was then a threat to the whole of Italy, he must remain allied with the other states – particularly Milan and Florence. Lodovico Sforza, though of a restless and ambitious nature, must have shared this view, because the danger from the Venetian senate threatened the rulers of Milan no less than the others and because it was easier for him to maintain the power he had usurped in the tranquillity of peace than in the vicissitudes of war . . . since there was the same will for peace in Ferdinand, Lodovico, and Lorenzo – partly for the same and partly for different reasons – it was easy to maintain an alliance in the name of Ferdinand, King of Naples, Giovan Galeazzo, Duke of Milan, and the Florentine Republic for the mutual defence of their states.

F. Guicciardini, *History of Italy*, written in the 1530s, trans. C. Grayson, (1964) New York, pp. 86-8

Giorgio Vasari, the historian of Italian art, was conscious of the need to explain as well as narrate, as his prefaces show (above, p. 43). An example of explanation in action from Vasari is his account of why the Florentines were pre-eminent in painting, which he puts into the mouth of the master of Perugino.

> His Master always made him the same answer, that men perfect in all the arts and especially in painting went to Florence more than to other places, and that this was because in that city men had three incentives. The first was the fact that many people were extremely critical, because the air was conducive to freedom of thought, and that men were not satisfied with mediocre works but had more care for the honour of the good and the beautiful than respect for their creators. Secondly, that it was necessary to be industrious in order to live, which meant using one's wits and judgement all the time, being quick, and finally knowing how to make a profit. For Florence did not have a large or fertile countryside round about it, so that men could not live cheaply there as they could in richer places. Thirdly, and perhaps just as important, was the greed for honour and glory which that air generates in men of every occupation. No man of spirit will allow men like himself to equal him, still less to leave him behind, even if he recognises them as masters. This greed for glory very often drives them to desire greatness so much that if they are not naturally wise or kindly, they turn out sharp-tongued, ungrateful and forgetful of benefits.
>
> G. Vasari, *Lives*, (1550), ed. G. Milanesi, volume III, (1887) Florence, pp. 567f

Not everyone agreed that explaining was the historian's business. Francesco Patrizzi, 1529-97, who was a professor of philosophy, thought that it was really the philosopher's job.

Patrizzi also wrote two books on Roman military history. His dialogues on history deserve a place near that of Bodin's *Methodus* (below pp. 84-5) in the history of historical method. In this dialogue Patrizzi figures himself, talking to Alfonso Bidernuccio.

> *Patrizzi.* Master Alfonso, do you know that it is for the philosophers to describe the causes of the things that happen in the world?
> *Bidernuccio.* I know: it is their job to do so.
> P. And you know that the effect comes from the cause, and not the other way round?
> B. I know this too . . .
> P. And that it is plausible to say that if a man knows the cause, he can know the effect too?

*B.* That's true.

*P.* If it is possible to know the cause and the effect separately, it is also possible for someone to know the cause and the effect together.

*B.* That's possible too.

*P.* Now we said that to know the cause was the job of the philosopher.

*B.* We did.

*P.* Whose job is it to know the case and the effect together?

*B.* That is the philosopher's job too, for the effect is joined to the cause.

*P.* But whose job is it to know the effect alone? . . . What would you call the writer who told you about the effects, without looking for any causes?

*B.* Do you by any chance want to say that this man is the historian?

*P.* You have said it.

F. Patrizzi, Ten dialogues on History, (1560)<br>Venice, ff.7-8

In spite of such opposition, the trend towards more and more historical explanation continued. Explanations imply generalisations, and a few historians (moving towards what we would call political science, or sociology, or social psychology) attempted to establish some. Here, for example, is part of Jean Bodin's social psychology, or if you prefer, his climatic theory of history. It is in a tradition which reaches back to Hippocrates and forward to Montesquieu. This passage may also help to make Vasari's remarks about the air of Florence (above, p. 83) less surprising, by showing that they were in fact part of a 'climate of opinion'.

> There would be no reason to impugn history, or to withhold agreement, if those who ought to have had the highest standards had had regard for truth and trustworthiness. Since, however, the disagreement among historians is such that some not only disagree with others but even contradict themselves, either from zeal or anger or error, we must make some generalisations as to the nature of all peoples or at least of the better known, so that we can test the truth of histories by just standards and make correct decisions about individual instances . . .
>
> Let us adopt this theory, that all who inhabit the area from the 45th parallel to the 75th toward the north grow increasingly warmer within, while the southerners, since they have more

warmth from the sun, have less from themselves . . . the strength of inward heat brings it about that those who live in northerly lands are more active and robust than the southerners. Even in the opposite area, beyond Capricorn's circle, the same thing happens: the further men move from the equator, the larger they grow, as in the land of the Patagonians, who are called giants, in the very same latitude as the Germans. This then, is the reason why Scythians have always made violent attacks southward; and what seems incredible, but is nevertheless true, the greatest empires always have spread southward – rarely from the south toward the north. The Assyrians defeated the Chaldeans; the Medes, the Assyrians; the Greeks, the Persians; the Parthians, the Greeks; the Romans, the Carthaginians; the Goths, the Romans; the Turks, the Arabs; and the Tartars, the Turks. The Romans, on the contrary, were unwilling to advance beyond the Danube. After Trajan had built a stone bridge of remarkable size across the Danube (for it is said that it had twenty pylons, of which the fragments even now remain), he did indeed conquer the Dacians completely. But when Hadrian understood that these tribes were not easily kept in subjection and did not submit to defeat, he ordered the bridge to be destroyed. Let us, however, cite more recent examples.

The French often suffered serious defeat at the hands of the English in France itself and almost lost their territory; they could never have penetrated into England, had they not been invited by the inhabitants. The English, on the other hand, were frequently overwhelmed by the Scots, and although they fought for control for more than 1200 years, yet they could not drive the Scots from a small part of the island, even when in resources and numbers they were as much superior to the Scots as they were inferior to the French.

> J. Bodin, *Method for the Easy Understanding of Histories*, (1566), trans. B. Reynolds, (1945) New York, pp. 85-93

Another approach made by Bodin to a generalised interpretation of history on an empirical basis (it is this basis which makes it different from interpretations offered by medieval writers like Otto of Freising, above p. 14) is a numerological one. This approach, unlike the climatic-geographical one, which gradually transformed itself into sociology, has turned out to be, if not a non-starter, at least a non-finisher. It is an interesting example of a Renaissance trend which does *not* announce the modern world. But it would give a one-sided view of Renaissance historical thought to leave this approach out, simply because it is not 'modern'.

It is remarkable that up to now, from all the Academicians, both Greek and Latin, no one has shown by the example of any state, that power and significance of numbers which relates to the type of empires. It is especially remarkable, since this concerns not only the type of government but also the growth, changes, and overthrow of states; it would even force the Epicureans to confess that human things are governed not recklessly and by chance, but by the majesty and providence of Almighty God . . . No one considering this matter attentively doubts that the death of men occurs in multiples of seven and nine: as 14, 18, 21, 27, 28, 35, 36, 42, 45, 49, 56. But if the seventh concurs with the ninth, all antiquity agreed that it was a most perilous year . . . for innumerable people die in the sixty-third year:[1] Aristotle, Chrysippus, Boccaccio, St. Bernard, Erasmus, Luther, Melanchthon, Silvius, Aleander, Jacob Sturm, Nicolas of Cusa, and Thomas Linacre . . .

If anyone should observe rather carefully the civil wars of the Romans, the secessions of the plebs, and the domestic strife, he would find that the number of years consists in sevens, or in nines, or in both. From the founding of the city to the flight of the kings, the years are 243; from the flight to the parricide, 468; from the flight to the secession of the plebs to the Sacred Mount, 18 years; to the second, 63; to the third, 225; to the sedition of the Gracchi, 378; from this to the Marian Civil War, 45; hence to the Caesarian War, 7; from the parricide to the civil war in Sicily, 7; hence to the last civil war, of Actium, 7. All these quantities are developed from whole nines or sevens or from both. Moreover, the town itself was captured 364 years after its founding, which is likewise formed from whole sevens; from the founding of the city until the defeat at Cannae, the years are 539, which is developed by taking 77 7 times. At that time the Roman Empire was nearly destroyed. From the disaster of Cannae to that of Barus, the years are 224. Both numbers are from whole sevens and both defeats occurred the second day of August. Likewise, Lysander leveled the walls of Athens to the ground in the 77th year after the victory of Salamis.

[1] This was the famous 'climacteric'.

Plutarch added in the life of Lysander that each happened on the sixth day of the month of *Munichion*. So also in the year of our Lord 707, in the seventh year of King Roderick, the Moors invaded Spain; in the 770th year thereafter they were driven forth, as may be read in Tarafa himself, a Spanish writer.

J. Bodin, *Method*, pp. 225-30

## 2  Cycles

Bodin's was an over-precise essay in the direction of a popular Renaissance interpretation of history, the cyclical. In the middle Ages, there had been more emphasis on the linear interpretation of history implicit in Christian doctrine. In the Renaissance, history being more concerned with this world, other patterns were discerned. The sixteenth century soldier-writer Luigi de Porto put forward a cyclical interpretation of history in epigrammatic form when he wrote that peace causes riches; riches, pride; pride, anger; anger, war; war, poverty; poverty, humility; humility, peace; peace, riches . . . and that is the way the world goes round (*così girano le cose del mondo*). Machiavelli, following Polybius, put forward a cyclical interpretation of political history, that the rule of a prince degenerates into a tyranny; this is replaced by a democracy, which degenerates into anarchy; then there is a prince again 'and this is the circle round which all states go' (*Discourses*, book 1, chapter 2). Again in his famous discussion of the three stages in the revival of the arts in Italy, Vasari seems to imply a cyclical theory of art history, for he knows that the ancients had been through all this before, and he recognised that after Michelangelo art 'has more reason to fear slipping back than to expect ever to make further advances'. Patrizzi in his *Ten Dialogues* suggests that all nations have beginnings, growth, maturity, decline and fall. By the early seventeenth century, this explanation is frequently invoked to account for the decline of Spain by Spaniards and foreigners alike. Sometimes it is suggested that states rise and fall because they (or nations, or the world) are like a man, who also grows, matures and decays. Sometimes the suggestion is that human affairs are subject to the influence of the moon, which also waxes and wanes. Whatever the image in which it is expressed (and these comparisons were not thought of as subjective but objective, not metaphors but genuine 'correspondences') the belief in historical cycles is very strong at this time. Here is one famous example, from a book devoted to the subject, Le Roy's *On the Vicissitude of Affairs*. Louis Le Roy, *c.* 1510-77, was a professor of Greek at the

Collège de France. Living between the French Renaissance and the Wars of Religion, he has a strong sense of the achievements of his age coupled with an apocalyptic vision of the future, which reinforced his general theory of cycles in history.

It is time to end this discourse which has clearly shown the vicissitude of all human affairs – arms, letters, languages, arts, states, laws, morals – and how they never cease rising and falling, growing better and worse alternately.

If the memory and knowledge of the past is the instruction of the present and the warning of the future, it is to be feared that having reached such great excellence, the power, wisdom, studies, books, industry, arts, and knowledge of the world will decline and be annihilated as they have been in the past. The order and perfection of today will be succeeded by confusion, civilisation by boorishness, knowledge by ignorance, elegance by barbarism. [With the mind's eye] I can already foresee various nations strange in shape, colour and dress, throwing themselves on Europe, as did once the Goths, Huns, Lombards, Vandals, and Saracens, They will destroy our towns, cities, castles, palaces, temples; change morals, laws, languages, and religion; they will burn libraries and destroy everything of beauty that they find in the countries that they occupy; in order to do away with their honour and virtue. I foresee foreign and civil wars everywhere; factions and heresies will arise which will profane everything divine and human; famines and plagues will threaten mortal men; the order of nature, the regular movements of the heavenly bodies, and the harmony of the elements will break apart, bringing floods, excessive heat, and most violent earthquakes. The universe will reach its end by one of these disorders, bringing with it confusion and the return of everything to its ancient chaos.

These things proceed, as the physicians say, from the law to which the world is subject; they have their natural causes. All the same, such happenings are dependent most of all on divine providence, which is higher than the whole of nature, and alone knows the appointed time when they must take place.

Louis Le Roy, On the Vicissitude of Affairs,<br>(1579) Paris, ff.112-13

In famous and eloquent passages, Francis Bacon and Thomas Browne expressed their belief in the cyclical interpretation of history.

In the youth of a state, arms do flourish; in the middle age of a

state, learning; and then both of them together for a time; in the
declining age of a state, mechanical arts and merchandise. Learning hath his infancy, when it is but beginning, and almost childish;
then his youth, when it is luxuriant and juvenile; then his strength
of years, when it is solid and reduced; and lastly his old age, when
it waxeth dry and exhaust. But it is not good to look too long
upon these turning wheels of vicissitude, lest we become giddy.

> Francis Bacon, *Essays*, ed. W. A. Wright,
> (1881) London, pp. 237-8; this essay first
> appears in the 1625 edition

As though there were a Metempsychosis, and the soul of one
man passed into another, opinions do find, after certain revolutions, men and minds like those that first begat them . . . men are
lived over again, the world is now as it was in ages past . . . because the glory of one state depends upon the ruin of another,
there is a revolution and vicissitude of their greatness, and must
obey the swing of that wheel, not moved by intelligences,[1] but
by the hand of God, whereby all estates arise to their zenith and
vertical parts according to their predestinated periods. For the
lives, not only of men, but of Commonwealths, and of the whole
world, run not upon a helix that still enlargeth, but on a circle,
where, according to their meridian, they decline on obscurity, and
fall under the horizon again.

> Sir Thomas Browne, *Religio Medici* written
> c. 1635, published 1642, (1906) London, pp.
> 8, 20-1

# 3  Unmasking and the Anatomy of Revolution

If some sixteenth-century historians invoked the stars, others kept
their eyes nearer the ground, and focussed on human motives, especially
that of self-interest. After Guicciardini, one of the great masters of this
type of explanation was the Venetian friar Paolo Sarpi, 1552-1623,
celebrated as the man who in his history 'unmasked' the Council of
Trent. 'Unmasking' meant showing that when men claimed to act
idealistically, they were really acting out of self-interest; it meant the
reduction of religious history to political. Politics were for Sarpi what
since Marx we have learned to call the 'infrastructure', the basic reality.
In the passage that follows he narrates the events leading up to Paul
III's decision to transfer the Council. But what he presents in narrative

[1] It was believed that the planets were moved by their souls, known as 'intelligences'.

form is a set of hypotheses put forward by Sarpi to explain the pope's action, and suggesting that Paul opposed attempts to reform the Church because they would lead to his losing power.

The pope thought about the news he had had from Trent and from his nuncio in Germany, and he discussed it with his intimates. He feared that the Council would bring forth some monstrosity to the prejudice of himself and the power of the papacy in general. He considered the theologians' factions, especially those of the Dominicans and Franciscans, ancient rivals and doctrinal opponents, who had been carried away at the Council and overstepped the limits which the prudent had laboriously set. The differences between them were no less than those with the Lutherans, and the controversy was as sharp, so that if they did not come to some understanding, there was a danger that something serious might happen. He thought particularly about the dispute whether residence was *de iure divino*, and about the daring of Brother Bartolomeo Carranza, who, egged on by many people, had gone so far as to call the contrary opinion a doctrine of the devil. He saw how easily another disease might arise, like that of Luther, and if residence were made a matter of faith, the papacy would be reduced to nothing. He considered that all the reforms had as their aim the limitation of the authority of the pope and the increase of that of the bishops. He had realised how little his authority was respected when the Council had given him hope of entrusting the task of reform to him (and he had even drawn up the bull, taking it all upon himself) and had then gone on discussing still more sharply without thinking about him. He greatly distrusted the liveliness and boldness of the Spaniards, having noticed that in general the Spaniards do not act at random, that they show greater respect than they feel, that they are closely united, and that they do not take a step without looking a hundred paces ahead. It seemed to him a most serious matter that they had met together and drawn up a censure in common. He thought it plausible that the emperor had suggested this, since his ambassador met them every day. He also suspected the intentions of the emperor because of his good fortune, which makes men unable to set limits on their plans. He considered the emperor's policy of toleration and explained it in terms of his wishing to curry favour with the Lutherans. He considered the complaints not only of the emperor, but of his ministers as well, when the Italian troops departed, that they had been abandoned in their time of need. He knew that the emperor blamed the duke of Piacenza (the Pope's son) for the rebellion of Genoa; and above all, he reflected on the emperor's words to the nuncio, that he had no greater enemy than the Pope. He feared that if the emperor were to obtain absolute power over Germany, he would then come to think of doing the same in Italy and use the Council as a weapon against the Pope. He saw that the emperor would have no rivals, given the incurable illness of the King of France, who was bound to die soon, and the fact that the Dauphin could not be counted on, being young and without experience. He was sure that the prelates who had supported the Curia up till now would declare for the emperor as soon as he came out openly against the Pope, whether out of fear, because the emperor was more powerful, or out of the universal envy of the Pope's authority – an envy which they would no longer hide once they saw that his authority could be limited in safety.

These considerations made him decide to do something about the Council. It did not seem possible to put an end to it, because of all the business that had still to be discussed. To suspend it he needed some important reason, and in any case this was not effective enough, because he would immediately be asked to raise the suspension. The best plan seemed to be the translation of the Council to a place over which he had absolute power. If this had to be done, it must be done in such a way as to remedy all dangers; this meant holding the Council in his own territories. Thinking about it, he decided that it would not be a good idea to hold it in Rome, because this would cause such a stir in Germany. Bologna seemed the best place, because it was large, fertile, and convenient for those who came from the other side of the Alps. Thinking along these lines, he decided to keep out of the affair personally, but to make it appear that the legates had done everything on their own initiative, by virtue of the authority which he had given them in the bull of February 22, which had been sent to them in August, 1545. In this way, if there was any opposition to the translation, the legates would bear the brunt of it, and he, as one who was not involved, could support them all the more easily. And if for some reason he changed his mind, he could do so without loss of face.

P. Sarpi, *History of the Council of Trent*, (1619), in *Sarpi*, ed. P. Burke, (1967) New York, book II, chapter 9, pp. 194-6

A different approach to the French wars of religion from Le Roy's, more in the tradition of Guicciardini, offering something more like a middle-range historical explanation, is provided by the beginning of Davila's *Civil Wars in France*, published in 1630, a generation after those wars were over. Arrigo Caterina Davila, 1576–1631, was a page to Catherine de'Medici and a professional soldier in the service of Henri IV and of Venice. One quality of his historical analysis, which makes it different from that of Guicciardini and other sixteenth-century writers, is that he is acutely aware, like many men of his generation, of the importance of hidden causes and feigned motives, of the difference between appearance and reality in history. One might call this awareness a 'baroque' sense of history, in that the art and literature of the baroque is also very much concerned with the exploration of the difference between appearance and reality. Whatever it is called, this awareness has permanently enriched historical analysis.

The civil wars, which for forty years together reduced the kingdom of France to disorder and misery, included such great enterprises that they are a marvellous source of useful lessons for anyone who considers them wisely. On the other hand, their progress was obscure and confused. The causes of many movements are not apparent; the motives for many decisions are not clear; and an infinite number of matters cannot be understood, because the interests of private individuals have been disguised under various pretexts. It is true that many excellent writers have tried hard to make this fruitful material more intelligible, and their great diligence and praiseworthy industry have resulted in important contributions to knowledge. The difficulties and obstacles are great, however; there is a multitude of events which are all noteworthy and all important, but they are buried under the tremendous ruins of the civil wars. And so a work which undertakes to excavate them and describe them in order will be no less valuable for the future than the works which have already been written in the past.

When I was a small child, I was taken to the central region of the kingdom of France, and I have lived there for a long time. Thanks to the course of my troubled life, I have therefore had the opportunity of observing with my own eyes both the most noteworthy and the most obscure circumstances of these famous events. I could not find more worthy material, or a better way of spending my time in my mature years than to apply myself to describing the progress of these troubles from their very beginning. The first armed clash came in 1560, before I was born, so that I was unable to be present at the beginning of the civil wars. However, I have contrived to be informed about it most thoroughly by the very persons who then governed the affairs of the kingdom. Thanks to this, and to my complete and exact knowledge of what came after, I have been able to penetrate with ease to the most ancient and the most remote causes of the wars . . .

In the execution of this difficult enterprise of mine, I shall not have the aid of a ready flow of words, or of grand concepts. However, I am free from the passions which generally lead writers astray, and so I hope to be able to follow the natural order and explanation of the events which I experienced for myself on the spot, since I spent many years in the chambers of kings and in the front line of armies.

A. C. Davila, *The Civil Wars in France*, (1630)
(1811 edition) Milan, pp. 3-5

England had to wait two more generations for its Davila, just as the English civil wars came two generations later than the French. The English Davila was Edward Hyde, Earl of Clarendon, 1609-74, who served both Charles I and Charles II. He wrote because he needed to explain the 'grounds, circumstances, and artifices' of the disaster which had happened to England, just as Davila and Guicciardini before him had had their powers of analysis stimulated by the psychological need to come to terms with, to account for disaster – a civil war and a foreign invasion. Clarendon combines a traditional, 'hand of God' explanation with the newer, more secular interest in secondary or 'natural' causes. Penetrating when it comes to giving explanations on an individual, personal level, Clarendon is also aware of the importance of more impersonal forces, which he refers to here as 'the temper, disposition, and habit of that time', but he does not care to analyse them further.

That posterity may not be deceived, by the prosperous wickedness of these times, into an opinion that less than a general combination, and universal apostasy in the whole nation from their religion and allegiance, could, in so short a time, have produced such a total and prodigious alteration and confusion over the whole kingdom; . . . it will not be unuseful, (at least to the curiosity if not the conscience of men,) to present to the world a full and clear narration of the grounds, circumstances, and artifices

of this Rebellion, not only from the time since the flame hath
been visible in a civil war, but looking farther back, from those
former passages, accidents, and actions, by which the seed plots
were made and framed from whence these mischiefs have succes-
sively grown to the height they are now at.

And then, though the hand and judgement of God will be very
visible, in the infatuating a people (as ripe and prepared for destruction) into all the perverse actions of folly and madness, making
the weak to contribute to the designs of the wicked, and suffering
even these by degrees, out of the conscience of their guilt, to grow
more wicked than they intended to be; letting the wise be imposed upon by men of no understanding, and possessing the innocent with laziness and sleep in the most visible article of danger;
uniting the ill, though of the most different opinions, divided
interests, and distant affections, in a firm and constant league of
mischief; and dividing those whose opinions and interests are the
same into faction and emulation, more pernicious to the public
than the treason of the others: whilst the poor people, under pretence of zeal to Religion, Law, Liberty, and Parliaments, (words
of precious esteem in their just signification,) are furiously hurried
into actions introducing Atheism, and dissolving all the elements
of Christian Religion, cancelling all obligations, and destroying
all foundations of Law and Liberty, and rendering not only the
privileges but very being of Parliaments desperate and impossible:
I say, though the immediate finger and wrath of God must be
acknowledged in these perplexities and distractions, yet he who
shall diligently observe the distempers and conjunctures of time,
the ambition, pride, and folly of persons, and the sudden growth
of wickedness, from want of care and circumspection in the first
impressions, will find all this bulk of misery to have proceeded,
and to have been brought upon us, from the same natural causes
and means which have usually attended kingdoms swoln with long
plenty, pride, and excess, towards some signal mortification, and
castigation of Heaven . . .

I shall not then lead any man farther back in this journey, for
the discovery of the entrance into these dark ways, than the
beginning of this King's reign. For I am not so sharp-sighted as
those who have discerned this rebellion contriving from, if not
before, the death of Queen Elizabeth, and fomented by several
Princes and great ministers of state in Christendom to the time
that it brake out. Neither do I look so far back as believing the

design to be so long since formed; (they who have observed the several accidents, not capable of being contrived, which have contributed to the several successes, and do know the persons who have been the grand instruments towards this change, of whom there have not been any four of familiarity and trust with each other, will easily absolve them from so much industry and fore-sight in their mischief;) but that, by viewing the temper, disposition, and habit, of that time, of the court and of the country, we may discern the minds of men prepared, of some to do, and of others to suffer, all that hath since happened: the pride of this man, and the popularity of that; the levity of one, and the morosity of another; the excess of the court in the greatest want, and the parsimony and retention of the country in the greatest plenty; the spirit of craft and subtlety in some, and the rude and unpolished integrity of others, too much despising craft or art; like so many atoms contributing jointly to this mass of confusion now before us.

> E. Hyde, *History of the Rebellion*, volume II,
> ed. W. D. Macray, (1881) Oxford, pp. 461-4

The philosopher Thomas Hobbes, 1588-1679, was another who tried to unravel the causes of the civil wars of England in his dialogue *Behemoth*, the historical counterpart to his more famous work of political theory, the *Leviathan* (1651).

*A*. If in time, as in place, there were degrees of high and low I verily believe that the highest of time would be that which passed between 1640 and 1660. For he that thence, as from the Devil's Mountain, should have looked upon the world and observed the actions of men, especially in England, might have had a prospect of all kinds of injustice, and of all kinds of folly, that the world could afford, and how they were produced by their hypocrisy and self-conceit, whereof the one is double iniquity, and the other double folly.

*B*. I should be glad to behold that prospect. You that have lived in that time and in that part of your age, wherein men used to see best into good and evil, I pray you set me, that could not see so well, upon the same mountain, by the relation of the actions you then saw, and of their causes, pretensions, justice, order, artifice, and event.

*A*. In the year 1640, the government of England was monarchical;

and the King that reigned, Charles, the first of that name, holding the sovereignty, by right of a descent continued above six hundred years, and from a much longer descent King of Scotland, and from the time of his ancestor Henry II, King of Ireland; a man that wanted no virtue, either of body or mind, nor endeavoured anything more than to discharge his duty towards God, in the well governing of his subjects.

*B.* How could he then miscarry, having in every country so many trained soldiers, as would, put together, have made an army of 60,000 men, and divers magazines of ammunition in places fortified?

*A.* If those soldiers had been, as they and all other of his subjects ought to have been, at his Majesty's command, the peace and happiness of the three kingdoms had continued as it was left by King James. But the people were corrupted generally, and disobedient persons esteemed the best patriots.

*B.* But sure there were men enough, besides those that were illaffected, to have made an army sufficient to have kept the people from uniting into a body able to oppose him.

*A.* Truly, I think, if the King had had money, he might have had soldiers enough in England. For there were very few of the common people that cared much for either of the causes, but would have taken any side for pay or plunder. But the King's treasury was very low, and his enemies, that pretended the people's ease from taxes, and other specious things, had the command of the purses of the city of London, and of most cities and corporate towns in England, and of many particular persons besides.

*B.* But how came the people to be so corrupted? And what kind of people were they that did so seduce them?

*A.* The seducers were of divers sorts. One sort were ministers; ministers, as they called themselves, of Christ; and sometimes, in their sermons to the people, God's ambassadors; pretending to have a right from God to govern every one his parish, and their assembly the whole nation.

Secondly, there were a very great number, though not comparable to the other, which notwithstanding that the Pope's power in England, both temporal and ecclesiastical, had been by Act of Parliament abolished, did still retain a belief that we ought to be governed by the Pope, whom they pretended to be the vicar of Christ, and, in the right of Christ, to be the governor of all Christian people. And these were known by the name of Papists;

as the ministers I mentioned before, were commonly called Presbyterians.

Thirdly, there were not a few, who in the beginning of the troubles were not discovered, but shortly after declared themselves for a liberty in religion, and those of different opinions one from another. Some of them, because they would have all congregations free and independent upon one another, were called Independents. Others that held baptism to infants, and such as understood not into what they are baptised, to be ineffectual, were called therefore Anabaptists. Others that held that Christ's kingdom was at this time to begin upon the earth, were called Fifth-Monarchy-men; besides divers other sects, as Quakers, Adamites, &c., whose names and peculiar doctrines I do not well remember. And these were the enemies which arose against his Majesty from the private interpretation of the Scripture, exposed to every man's scanning in his mother-tongue.

Fourthly, there were an exceeding great number of men of the better sort, that had been so educated, as that in their youth having read the books written by famous men of the ancient Grecian and Roman commonwealths concerning their policy and great actions; in which books the popular government was extolled by that glorious name of liberty, and monarchy disgraced by the name of tyranny; they became thereby in love with their forms of government. And out of these men were chosen the greatest part of the House of Commons, or if they were not the greatest part, yet by advantage of their eloquence, were always able to sway the rest.

Fifthly, the city of London and other great towns of trade, having in admiration the prosperity of the Low Countries after they had revolted from their monarch, the King of Spain, were inclined to think that the like change of government here, would to them produce the like prosperity.

Sixthly, there were a very great number that had either wasted their fortunes, or thought them too mean for the good parts they thought were in themselves; and more there were, that had able bodies, but saw no means how honestly to get their bread. These longed for a war, and hoped to maintain themselves hereafter by the lucky choosing of a party to side with, and consequently did for the most part serve under them that had greatest plenty of money.

Lastly, the people in general were so ignorant of their duty, as that no one perhaps of ten thousand knew what right any man had to command him, or what necessity there was of King or Commonwealth, for which he was to part with his money against his will; but thought himself to be so much master of whatsoever he possessed, that it could not be taken from him upon any pretence of common safety without his own consent. King, they thought, was but a title of the highest honour, which gentleman, knight, baron, earl, duke, were but steps to ascend to, with the help of riches; they had no rule of equity, but precedents and custom; and he was thought wisest and fittest to be chosen for a Parliament, that was most averse to the granting of subsidies or other public payments.

> T. Hobbes, *Behemoth*, in *English Works*, ed. Sir William Molesworth, volume VI, (1840) London, pp. 165f.

England was not the only country to live through a revolution in the mid-seventeenth century; there was a wave of revolts in Europe in the 1640s. Similarly, England was not the only country where revolution was anatomised; in Italy in particular, there was a whole crop of books which tried to explain recent 'commotions' as well as to describe them. The actual word 'revolution' (*revolutio* in Latin, *revolutione* in Italian) now took on a political meaning, whereas it had previously been an astronomical term, as in Copernicus's *Revolutions of the Celestial Orbs*. In Italy, Giraffi applied the term in 1647 to the revolt in Naples of that year; in England, Matthew Wren referred to 'the revolution in England' about the year 1650. The reason for the adoption of the term is probably the belief in historical cycles, discussed above.

Of the various writers who discuss the revolts of the 1640s, one of the most interesting is count Maiolino Bisaccioni, 1582-1663, a nobleman from Ferrara who turned professional writer and settled in Venice. The opening of his book places him in the tradition of Machiavelli and the seventeenth-century writers on Tacitus and reason of state.

> Among the different classes of people for whom history is useful (it is entertaining for everyone), no one should cultivate the study (I shall not say just the knowledge) of it more than the Prince. This is because history is a narrative of the actions of princes and great men, and one learns from those who are like oneself; it is also because history is the true mistress of the art of governing states, and shows what courses of actions to pursue, which to avoid openly, and which to evade in a more subtle manner. I distin-

guished reading history from studying it, because a work of history written by a man of understanding has a more juicy marrow than a simple narrative of facts. Hence Cornelius Tacitus has a greater reputation than other historians much more learned than he. He does not only describe what happened, but so to speak, he writes a commentary on his own narrative, and allows the reader to penetrate more deeply into events of which he merely suggests an interpretation. But if any history is of value for princes, the most useful, believe me, is that which tells of the revolutions and commotions of peoples [*le revolutioni, o commotioni de' popoli*] . . . revolutions usually spring from bad government by ministers. And so I have come to write of the many popular revolts [*rivolte de' popoli*] which have happened in my time, which might reasonably be called Political Earthquakes . . .

M. Bisaccioni, *History of the Recent Civil Wars*,
(2nd edition, 1653), pp. 1-2

Bisaccioni goes on to describe these political earthquakes one by one, beginning with England and going on to Catalonia. His account of the Catalans introduces some important distinctions between internal and external, manifest and hidden causes, which remind one that Bisaccioni belonged to the same generation as Davila. His aim, he declares,

is to describe this war, which had two causes, one internal, and the other external. Of the first, we shall speak later. As for the second, I have something to say here, so as not to mix it up with the other . . . [he describes how churches in Catalonia were sacked by German mercenaries]. The Catalans thought that they had to take up arms to chase these incendiaries from their country and these image-breakers from their churches.

The second external cause was the extraordinary billettings, in the manner of Lombardy. The Catalans complained that not only was their property consumed, but they were ill-treated themselves into the bargain . . .

It is extremely difficult to penetrate the hearts of men, and above all those of princes. The man who claims to be best informed is often the most deceived; for it is very true that *cor regis in manu Dei* [the king's heart is in the hand of God] and that thousands of folds cover the deepest secrets. These princes, very often, try to achieve their ends by hiding them from their own councillors, and invent other, apparent aims. This is true political prudence, thanks to the

unfaithfulness of ministers, who, moved by love or hate, avarice
or ambition (the four corners of prevarication), reveal the secrets
of their rulers. And so it has become an essential rule to deceive
the minister for the sake of self-interest. If, then, the intentions of
princes are known to God alone, it is no wonder that I, in the
beginning of this account of Catalan affairs, am not so presump-
tuous as to deal with the truest causes, but deal only with the
apparent ones. It is not unknown to me that others (perhaps
maliciously) suggest that the number and importance of the
privileges of Catalonia, and especially of Barcelona, privileges
which the Catalans defend tenaciously, made some great minister
of the Most Catholic King think of diminishing them little by
little and so annihilating them – for just as material things are
destroyed by use, so immaterial ones are destroyed by lack of it.
This theory is plausible (even if it is wrong), because these privileges made the Catalans seem to compete with the authority of the
prince, and in our day, which might be called the full moon of
monarchies, such rights are not pleasing to princes; rights which
were conceded when kings were more like first citizens than like
lords, and more like fathers of their country than like owners of it
. . . I know that the Catalans have always loved these privileges of
theirs so much that they hug them tightly and like jealous lovers,
suspect dangers where there are none . . . However, whatever
were the most remote causes of the troubles, it is enough for us to
know this, which is the truth, that in the year 1632 the king went
to hold the Estates in Barcelona, and that the Count-Duke
[Olivares], his chief minister, treated the deputies of that city with
such contempt (whether spontaneously or deliberately, I do not
know) that they began to see him as an enemy.

> M. Bisaccioni, *History of the Recent Civil Wars*,
> (2nd edition, 1653), pp. 1-2

It has been remarked more than once that some mid-seventeenth-
century authors seem to anticipate the economic and social interpretation of history usually believed to have been invented (or is it discovered?) in the course of the eighteenth and nineteenth centuries. In
the passages I have quoted, Hobbes suggests that English merchants
thought that, like the Dutch, they would be more prosperous under a
republic: Bisaccioni says that the Catalans were annoyed at the damage
done to their property by the billetting of troops: and Clarendon notes
'the excess of the court in the greatest want, and the parsimony and

retention of the country in the greatest plenty'. Clarendon, indeed goes still further in this direction in other passages; as Christopher Hill observes, he 'makes no bones about describing the line-up in the Civil War as a class division'. What Clarendon actually writes is the following. In Yorkshire,

> the Parliament party . . . plainly discerned that by much the greatest part of the persons of honour, quality and interest in the country would cordially oppose their proceedings: for, besides the lord Fairfax, there were in truth few of good reputation and fortune who ran that way . . . [whereas] Leeds, Halifax and Bradford, three very populous and rich towns (which depending wholly on clothiers naturally maligned the gentry), were wholly at their disposition.
>
> E. Hyde, *History of the Rebellion*, ed. W. D. Macray, (1888) Oxford, volume II, pp. 461, 464

Still closer to a general economic and social interpretation of history (as R. H. Tawney once pointed out in a celebrated lecture) is another mid-century anatomist of revolution, James Harrington, 1611-77. He argued for example that the balance of power between king and barons in English history depended on the balance of land, thus combining a Renaissance Italian approach to politics with the lawyers' discovery of feudal society. In the following passage he summarises the course of English history from 'Turbo' to 'Coraunus'.

> The monarchy of the Teutons [Anglo-Saxons] had stood in this posture about two hundred and twenty years when Turbo, Duke of Neustria [William, Duke of Normandy], making his claim to the crown of one of their kings that died childless, followed it with successful arms. And being possessed of the kingdom, used it as conquered, distributing the earldoms, thanelands, bishoprics, and prelacies of the whole realm among his Neustrians. From this time the earl came to be called *comes, consul* and *dux* (though *consul* and *dux* grew afterward out of use). The king's thanes came to be called barons, and their lands baronies . . . For barons, they came from henceforth to be in different times of three kinds: barons by their estates and tenures, barons by writ, and barons created by letters patent. From Turbo the first to Adoxus [King John] the seventh king from the conquest, barons had their denomination from their possessions and tenures, and these were either spiritual

or temporal. For not only the thanelands, but the possessions of bishops as also of some 26 abbots and two priors were now erected into baronies, whence the lords spiritual that had suffrage in the Teuton parliament as spiritual lords came to have it in the Neustrian parliament as barons and were made subject, which they had not formerly been, unto knight's service in chief. Barony coming henceforth to signify all honourary possessions as well spiritual as temporal, having right to sit in parliament, the baronies in this sense were sometimes more and sometimes fewer, but commonly about 200 or 250, containing in them a matter of sixty thousand *feuda militum* or knight's fees, whereof some twenty-eight thousand were in the clergy. It is ill luck that no man can tell what the land of a knight's fee (reckoned in some writs as forty pounds a year and in others at ten) was certainly worth; for by such a help we might have exactly demonstrated the *balance* of this *government* . . . the balance and foundation of this government was in the sixty thousand knight's fees, and these being possessed by the 250 lords, it was a *government* of the *few* or of the *nobility*, wherein the people might also assemble, but could have no more than a mere name. And the clergy holding a third to the whole nation, as is plain by the parliament roll, it is an absurdity (seeing the clergy of France came first through their riches to be a state of that kingdom) to acknowledge the people to have been a state of this realm and not allow it unto the clergy, who were so much more weighty in the balance, which is that of all other whence a state of order in a government is denominated. Wherefore this monarchy consisted of the king and of the three estates (or *ordines regni*), the lords spiritual and temporal, and the commons. It consisted of these, I say, as to the balance, though during the reign of some of these kings not as to the administration.

For the ambition of Turbo and some of those that more immediately succeeded him to be absolute princes strove against the nature of their foundation, and inasmuch as he had divided almost the whole realm among his Neustrians, with some encouragement for a while. But the Neustrians, while they were but foreign plants having no security against the natives but in growing up by their prince's sides, were no sooner well rooted in their vast dominions than they came up, according to the infallible consequence of the balance domestic, and contracting the national interest of the baronage grew as fierce in the vindication of the ancient rights and liberties of the same as if they had been always natives. Whence, the kings being as obstinate on the one side for their absolute power as these on the other for their immunities, grew certain wars which took their denomination from the barons . . . Dicotome (Richard II), being the twelfth king from the conquest, began to make barons by letters patent with the addition of honorary pensions for the maintenance of their dignities to them and their heirs, so that they were hands in the king's purse and had no shoulders for his throne . . . the old barons, taking Dicotome's prodigality to such creatures so ill that they deposed him, got the trick of it, and never gave over setting up and pulling down of their kings according to their various interests, and that faction of the White and Red into which they had been thenceforth divided, till Panurgus [Henry VII] the eighteenth king from the conquest was more by their favour than his right advanced to the crown. This king through his natural subtlety, reflecting at once upon the greatness of their power and the inconstancy of their favor, began to find another flaw in this kind of government, which is also noted by Machiavelli, namely, that a throne supported by a nobility is not so hard to be ascended as kept warm. Wherefore his secret jealousy lest the dissension of the nobility, as it brought him in, might throw him out, travelled in ways undiscovered by them unto ends as little foreseen by himself . . . Now that Panurgus in abating the power of the nobility was the cause whence it came to fall into the hands of the people appears by those several statutes that were made in his reign, as that for population, those against retainers, and that for alienations . . .

To this it happened that Coraunus [Henry VIII] the successor of that king, dissolving the abbeys brought with the declining estate of the nobility so vast a prey to the industry of the people that the balance of the commonwealth was too apparently in the popular party to be unseen by the wise counsel of Queen Parthenia [Queen Elizabeth] who, converting her reign through the perpetual love tricks that passed between her and her people into a kind of romance, wholly neglected the nobility. And by these degrees came the House of Commons to raise that head which since has been so high and formidable to their princes that they have looked pale upon those assemblies.

> J. Harrington, *Oceana*, (1656) London, 'the second part of the preliminaries'

Despite this passage it seems that in the seventeenth century, a true economic or social interpretation of history never quite appears, any more than a monograph on economic or social history; for Harrington's framework is political-legal, and Clarendon's observations about social groups are too rare, too marginal to his thought. The true 'infrastructure', for the seventeenth-century mind, is not economy or society; not even politics or law: it is God. Ralegh, in his *History of the World*, argued that God made kingdoms prosperous or wretched according to their deserts. Clarendon, in his *Reflections* on the Psalms, expected divine judgement on the 'violent party', which would take the form of dividing them, as the rebels against King David had been divided. Bossuet, in his *Discourse on Universal History* (1681) explained the rise and fall of empires in terms of the purposes of God. Preaching to the House of Commons in 1640, Stephen Marshall, a puritan divine, told the House that it was nothing but God's instrument:

> the hand of the dial makes not the clock to go but shows how it doth go.

> Sermon, preached 17 November 1640, (1645)
> London, p. 23

# V

# NARRATIVE

During the Renaissance, history was often thought of as a branch of rhetoric. Form was sometimes thought of as more important than content; a good style more important than an interest in what had actually happened, or why. The Spanish Jesuit Mariana, 1535-1625, admits as much about his popular *History of Spain*.

> I never undertook to make a history of Spain in which I should verify every particular fact; for if I had, I should never have finished it; but I undertook to arrange in a becoming style and in the Latin language what others had collected as materials for the fabric I desired to raise.
>
> > Mariana, Letter to Argensola, trans, in G. Lewy, *Constitutionalism and Statecraft*, (1960) Geneva, p. 25

In general Renaissance literature differs from later medieval literature in that it is concerned to a great extent with structure, with formal organisation. Whatever was written ought, so it was believed, to conform to a specific genre, preferably one that existed in classical antiquity, and imitate the masters in that genre. A historian ought to follow Livy or Thucydides, just as an epic poet ought to follow Homer and Vergil. An epic should deal with heroic adventures; begin in the middle; and contain scenes set in Heavens as well as on Earth. A history should also deal with heroic actions; anything less was beneath the 'dignity of history', a phrase which was much used at the Renaissance. The dignity of history, for the Renaissance writer as for Tacitus (below, p. 133) excluded 'low' people, things, or words.[1] According to the French Jesuit Rapin, 1621-87, Caesar had offended against this rule because

the military machines of Caesar are described in his Commentaries

[1] Compare the tsar's remark to Pushkin on hearing that he was planning to write about Pugachev, the eighteenth-century Russian peasant leader, 'such a man has no history'.

with too great a particularity of circumstances in a subject so
mechanic as that is.

R. Rapin, *Critical works*, English trans., (1706)
London, p. 72

An exact analogy to this way of thinking can be found in the art
theory of the sixteenth and seventeenth centuries. Poussin declared that
the subject-matter of painting should be noble or lofty, such as battles
or heroic actions. In a picture of the Flight into Egypt Poussin left out
the camels mentioned in the Bible because they were beneath the
dignity of the history. The prejudice was part literary, part social.
According to the classical rule of the separation of styles, revived at the
Renaissance, anything 'low' or belonging to everyday life had to be
treated in the low style, while the historian usually wrote in the high
style; but this literary value was obviously the reflection of a social one.
The consequences of this prejudice were extremely important; it dis-
torted political history, as Descartes pointed out, and it prevented social
history from emerging at all until the eighteenth century – at the same
time, interestingly enough, as the emergence of *genre* painting in France
and England.

The influence of rhetoric was apparent on what was put into the
Renaissance history, as well as what was omitted. Histories usually
contained set-pieces which gave the author a chance to show off his
rhetorical skill. There set-pieces included the 'character', or moral
portrait of an outstanding individual; the description of action, particularly of a battle; and, most important of all, the speech. In all three
cases there was a danger that beauty, or the desire to imitate an ancient
historian, might conquer truth. Characters, battles and speeches tended
to assume stereotyped forms, just as painters tended to imitate classical
gestures and poets to follow classical *topoi*. What mattered to the
Renaissance historian was not to convey any precise indication of the
individuality of *this* man, or to describe precisely what was said or done
on *this* occasion, but to give a general impression of *a* leader, *a* battle,
*an* oration. If the evidence was not available, it was permissible – here
is the rub – to invent. One might be unable to find out whether the
French attacked the left wing or the right, but it was always possible
to describe lances and horses, brave assaults and greed for plunder. It
would almost certainly be impossible to discover what a general said
to his troops on a specific occasion, if indeed he addressed them at all;
but it was always possible to produce a 'hortatory oration'. The reading
public liked this; the evidence is the fact that anthologies of speeches

from leading historians, ancient and modern, were published. For example, in 1573 François de Belleforêt published a book of 1434 pages called *Military Harangues*, the speeches selected from famous historians and each preceded by a summary of the argument and followed by an account of its effect. One has to remember that Renaissance humanists had enormous confidence in the power of rhetoric to win battles, take fortresses, and change the form of government of states.

Let me now offer some examples of these humanist set-pieces. First of all, three 'characters', from Commynes, Guicciardini, and Clarendon.

Philippe de Commynes, 1447-1511, was in the service of Charles the Bold, then deserted to Louis XI. He wrote his memoirs between 1489 and 1498. It may be thought odd to call him a 'humanist' historian, as he could hardly write Latin, and his work can be located in the Froissart tradition; but some classical learning seems to have rubbed off on him, and he is reminiscent of Livy as well as of Froissart.

> Of all the princes I have ever known, the most skilful at extricating himself from a tight place when affairs were going badly was our master King Louis XI. He was also the most simple in words and in dress, and the one who worked hardest to win over a man who could be of use to him or do him harm. He would not be annoyed by a rebuff from a man he was trying to win over, but went on making generous promises and giving him money and offices which the king knew would please him. The men he had dismissed in time of peace and prosperity he bought back at a high price when he needed them; and he made use of them and bore no grudge against them for what had happened.
>
> He was naturally the friend of people of middle rank (*moyen estat*) and the enemy of all the great, who did not need him. There was never man who listened to as many people, or enquired about as many matters, or wished to know as many men as he; for he knew everyone of importance in England, Spain, Portugal and Italy and the lands of the duke of Burgundy and Britanny just as well as he knew his own subjects. These habits of his which I have mentioned were the saving of his crown, considering the enemies he had acquired by succeeding to it.
>
> Above all, his great liberality was of use to him. However, just as he was wise in adversity, so in the opposite situation, when he thought himself safe or in time of truce, he began to annoy people in little ways which did not do him any good; he could scarcely

endure peace. He was not careful of what he said about people, whether they were present or absent, except those he feared: there were many of these, for he was by nature quite a timorous man. When he had done himself some harm by speaking in this way, or feared that he had done so, and wished to make amends, he would speak as follows to the man concerned: 'I know well that my tongue has done me great harm, just as it has sometimes given me much pleasure. All the same, it is right that I should make amends.' Whenever he said this he would give some present to the man to whom he spoke, and it would not be a small one.

God gives a prince great grace when he knows good from evil, especially when there is more good, as in the case of this king our master. But it is my opinion that the hardships of his youth, when he had fled from his father to Duke Philip of Burgundy, at whose court he passed six years, were of great value to him, for he was forced to please the people of whom he had need. This gave him the experience of adversity, which is no small thing.

P. de Commynes, Memoirs, ed. J. Calmette,<br>(1924) Paris, volume I, book I, chapter 10

Francesco Guicciardini, 1483-1540, was a Florentine patrician and an administrator in papal service. He was much more steeped in the classics than Commynes and this character of pope Alexander seems to echo Livy on Hannibal (p. 131, below).

Innocent was followed by Rodrigo Borgia of Valencia, one of the royal cities of Spain. A senior cardinal and a leading figure at the court of Rome, he was raised to the papacy, however, by the disagreements between the cardinals Ascanio Sforza and Giuliano di san Piero in Vincola, and more by the fact that setting a new example in that age, he openly bought, partly with money and partly with promises of offices and favours he would bestow, many of the cardinals' votes. It is well known that the King of Naples, though in public he hid his grief, told his wife with tears – which he was unaccustomed to shed even at the death of his children – that a pope had been elected who would be fatal to Italy and the whole Christian world: truly a prophecy not unworthy of the wisdom of Ferdinand. For Alexander VI (as the new pope wished to be called) possessed remarkable sagacity and acumen, excellent counsel, marvellous powers of persuasion and incredible ability and application in all difficult enterprises; but these virtues were far outweighed by his vices: utterly obscene habits, neither sincerity

nor shame nor truth nor faith nor religion, insatiable avarice, immoderate ambition, more than barbarous cruelty and a burning
desire to advance his many children in any possible way.

> F. Guicciardini, *History of Italy*, trans. C.
> Grayson, (1964) New York, pp. 89-90

A third character, mid-seventeenth century but still in the humanist
tradition, is this one of Laud by Clarendon.

He was a man of great parts, and very exemplar virtues, allayed
and discredited by some unpopular natural infirmities; the greatest
of which was (besides a hasty, sharp way of expressing himself,)
that he believed innocence of heart and integrity of manners was
a guard strong enough to secure any man in his voyage through
this world, in what company soever he travelled and through what
ways soever he was to pass: and sure never any man was better
supplied with that provision. He was born of honest parents, who
were well able to provide for his education in the schools of learning, from whence they sent him to St. John's college in Oxford,
the worst endowed at that time of any in that famous university.
From a scholar he became a fellow, and then the president of that
college, after he had received all the graces and degrees, the proc-
torship and the doctorship, that could be obtained there. He was
always maligned and persecuted by whose who were of the
Calvinian faction, which was then very powerful, and who,
according to their useful maxim and practice, call every man they
do not love, Papist; and under this senseless appellation they
created him many troubles and vexations, and so far suppressed
him that, though he was the King's chaplain and taken notice of
for an excellent preacher and a scholar of the most sublime parts,
he had not any preferment to invite him to leave his poor college,
which only gave him bread, till the vigour of his age was past . . .
When he came into great authority, it may be he retained too
keen a memory of those who had so unjustly and uncharitably
persecuted him before, and, I doubt, was so far transported with
the same passions he had reason to complain of in his adversaries,
that, as they accused him of Popery because he had some doctrinal
opinions which they liked not, though they were nothing allied
to Popery, so he entertained too much prejudice to some persons
as if they were enemies to the discipline of the Church, because
they concurred with Calvin in some doctrinal points, when they

abhorred his discipline, and reverenced the government of the Church, and prayed for the peace of it with as much zeal and fervency as any in the kingdom; as they made manifest in their lives, and in their sufferings with it and for it. He had, from his first entrance into the world, without any disguise or dissimulation, declared his own opinion of that *Classis* of men; and as soon as it was in his power he did all he could to hinder the growth and increase of that faction, and to restrain those who were inclined to it from doing the mischief they desired to do. But his power at Court could not enough qualify him to go through with that difficult reformation whilst he had a superior in the Church, who, having the reins in his hand, could slacken them according to his own humour and indiscretion, and was thought to be the more remiss to irritate his choleric disposition. But when he had now the primacy in his own hand, the King being inspired with the same zeal, he thought he should be to blame, if he did not make haste to apply remedies to those diseases which he saw would grow apace.

> E. Hyde, Earl of Clarendon, *History of the Rebellion*, ed. W. D. Macray, (1888) Oxford, volume I, pp. 120-2

Humanist 'characters' were the literary equivalent of state portraits; Guicciardini the equivalent of Titian. The second set-piece, the battle-scene, was even more like a Renaissance picture (which was itself often called a 'history', *istoria*). Battle-scenes were a favourite Renaissance subject (Uccello's battle of San Romano, Piero della Francesca's Triumph of Constantine) and humanist battle-pieces were like them in that they were usually generalised descriptions much of which could refer to any battle. A comparison will bring this out: Guicciardini's description of the battle of Fornovo, and Vasari's description of Leonardo's lost painting of the battle of Anghiari. They both make the same rhetorical point, about the horses fighting with their teeth, a point no more likely to have been true of one battle than another. Perhaps Guicciardini's description was influenced by the painting, which he could have seen some 25 years before he wrote.

> He showed a group of horsemen fighting for a standard, in a drawing which was regarded as very fine and successful because of the wonderful ideas he expressed in his interpretation of the battle. In the drawing, rage, fury, and vindictiveness are displayed both by the men and by the horses, two of which with their

forelegs interlocked are battling with their teeth no less fiercely than their riders are struggling for the standard, the staff of which has been grasped by a soldier who, as he turns and spurs his horse to flight, is trying by the strength of his shoulders to wrest it by force from the hands of four others. Two of them are struggling for it with one hand and attempting with the other to cut the staff with their raised swords; and an old soldier in a red cap roars out as he grips the staff with one hand and with the other raises a scimitar and aims a furious blow to cut off both the hands of those who are gnashing their teeth and ferociously defending their standard.

Vasari, *Lives*, trans G. Bull, (1965) pp. 207-8

The French army spent a very troubled night because the Italians kept sending their *stradiotti* right up to their tents so that there were frequent calls to arms in their camp, which was in turmoil at every noise; then came a sudden and very heavy rainfall with fearful peals of thunder and terrible flashes of lightning – which seemed an augury of some dreadful disaster. This frightened the French much more than the Italian army, not only because, being surrounded by mountains and the enemy and in a place where if any disaster occurred they had no hope of escape, they were in a much more difficult position and had just cause to be more afraid; but also because it seemed more likely that the threats of heaven, which usually show themselves only for some great occasion, must point rather to the camp which held a king of such power and dignity.

The next morning, July 6th, the French army began to cross the river at dawn. Most of the artillery went first, followed by the vanguard. The King had included in this force, thinking that it would have to bear the brunt of the enemy's attack, 300 French lances, Gianiacopo da Tribulzio with his 100 lances, and 3,000 Swiss who were the mainstay and hope of the army. And with them on foot Englebert, brother of the Duke of Cleves, and the Bailli of Dijon who had enlisted them; and to these the King added 300 archers on foot and some mounted crossbowmen from his own guard and nearly all the remaining infantry he had with him. Behind the vanguard came the main force with the King himself in its midst, fully armed and mounted on a mettlesome charger; and beside him to command this part of the army with his authority and advice M. de Trémouille, a very famous captain in the Kingdom of France. Behind them followed the rearguard led by the Comte de Foix, and finally the transport wagons. Nevertheless, not being averse to reaching an agreement, the King asked Argenton to go and negotiate with the Venetians at the very moment when his army began to move. But at the time of this move the Italian army was already up in arms and its captains had decided to fight and the time was too short and the armies too near to allow room or opportunity for talking. The light cavalry were already skirmishing on all sides, the artillery firing everywhere with terrible effect and the Italians had already come out of their camp and were deploying their squadrons ready for battle on the bank of the river. The French did not, however, halt their advance. Part of them were on the riverbed, and part, because they could not deploy their ranks on the narrow plain, on the lower slopes of the hill; and when the vanguard was right in front of the enemy camp, the Marquis of Mantua crossed the river behind the French rearguard with a squadron of 600 picked men-at-arms, a large force of *stradiotti* and 5,000 infantry, leaving on the farther bank Antonio da Montefeltro, the natural son of the late Federigo Duke of Urbino, with a large squadron ready to cross when called to reinforce the first assault. He had also arranged that when they had begun to fight, another section of the light cavalry should strike at the enemy's flank and that the rest of the *stradiotti*, crossing the river at Fornovo, should attack the French transport wagons. These had been left without guards – exposed to any one wishing to plunder them – either through lack of troops or (as it was rumored) on the advice of Tribulzio.

The Count of Gaiazzo with 2,000 foot soldiers and 400 men-at-arms, among them the company of Don Alfonso d'Este, which had come into camp without him at his father's request, crossed the Taro at another place to attack the French vanguard, leaving Annibale Bentivoglio on the farther shore with 200 men-at-arms to assist when called for. There remained two large companies of men-at-arms and 1,000 foot soldiers to guard the camp, because the Venetian commissioners wished to retain some safe protection for themselves against all eventualities. When the King saw so great a force attacking his rearguard contrary to his captains' expectations, he turned his back on the vanguard and began to lead his main force to support the rearguard, moving so rapidly himself with one squadron before the others that when the attack began he was among the first of his men in the front line. Some have recorded that the forces of the Marquis did not cross the river without some disorder because of the height of the banks and the obstacles provided by the trees, roots and branches which commonly cover the banks of torrents. Others add that his foot soldiers, because of these difficulties and of the waters swollen by the night's rain, were delayed in reaching the battle and did not all cross, not a few remaining on the other side of the river. Whatever the reason, it is certain that the Marquis' attack was very fierce and furious, and was met with like ferocity and courage. The squadrons entered the battle from all sides in a melée and not according to the custom of the wars of Italy, which was to fight, one squadron against another, and to replace this with another when the first was worsted or began to fall back, and not to make up one large squadron from several small ones except as a last resort. As a result the battles, in which very few men were ever killed, usually lasted nearly all day and were often brought to an end by nightfall without certain victory on either side.

When the lances were broken, many men-at-arms and horses fell to the ground in the encounter, and then they all began to wield with like ferocity maces, short swords and other small arms, the horses fighting with kicks, bites and blows no less than the men. Certainly at the beginning the Italians showed splendid courage thanks largely to the fighting spirit of the Marquis who, followed by a brave company of young noblemen and *lancie spezzate* (these are picked soldiers maintained outside the ordinary companies), and promptly affronting all dangers, did not lack any quality proper to a very valiant captain. The French bravely withstood this ferocious onslaught; but being hard pressed by a much superior force, they were already almost visibly beginning to fall back, thereby endangering the King. In fact a few steps away from him the bastard Bourbon was taken prisoner though fighting fiercely. At this the Marquis hoped to have the same success with the King himself, who had rashly moved himself into a position of great danger without the guard and precautions suitable to so great a prince. The Marquis made great efforts to get near Charles with a large number of his troops. The King with few of his men about him, showed great courage and defended himself nobly against the Marquis' attack more by the ferocity of his charger than the help of his soldiers. In such danger he did not lack those thoughts which fear usually brings to mind in difficult situations.

He saw himself almost abandoned by his men and turned to heaven for help and vowed to St. Denis and St. Martin – reputed to be the special protectors of the Kingdom of France – that if he got through safely with his army into Piedmont, he would go as soon as he returned to France to visit with rich gifts the churches dedicated to their names, one near Paris, the other at Tours, and that every year he would bear witness with solemn feasts and offerings to the grace he had received through them. When he had made these vows his strength renewed and he began to fight more vigorously than seemed possible for a man of his strength and physique. But the King's danger had so roused those who were not far away that they all hastened to protect his royal person and they held back the Italians. At this moment his company, which had been left behind, came up; and one squadron fiercely attacked the enemy on the flank, which curbed their impetus a good deal. Then Ridolfo da Gonzaga, the uncle of the Marquis of Mantua, a commander of great experience – while urging on his men and reforming them wherever their ranks were beginning to break and moving here and there doing the work of an excellent captain – chanced to raise his visor and was wounded in the face by a Frenchman's sword and fell from his horse. His own men and horses falling on top of him he was rather suffocated in the crush than killed by enemy arms. It was certainly an end unworthy of him because in the discussions the day before and that same morning he had thought it imprudent to risk so much unnecessarily. He had advised, against his nephew's wishes, that they should avoid a battle.

As the battle swayed one way and the other and neither the Italians nor the French appeared to gain any advantage, it was more doubtful than ever who would be the victor. So as fear and hope ran equal on both sides, they fought with unbelievable ardor, every man feeling that victory lay in his right hand and in his valor. The courage of the French was stimulated by the presence and the danger of their King – for the King's majesty is venerated among that nation by ancient custom no less than the name of God – and by the fact that they were in a position where only victory could save them. The Italians were encouraged by the greed for plunder, the ferocity and example of the Marquis, their success in the early part of the fight and the great number of their army, so that they could expect help from many on their own side. The French could have no such hopes because their forces were either all engaged in the fighting or expected at any moment to be attacked by the enemy. But in all human actions (as everyone knows) the power of fortune is enormous – greater in military affairs than in any others; but immeasurable, immense, infinite in deed of arms, where an order misunderstood, a maneuver badly executed, a rash move, a vain cry even from a simple soldier, often brings victory to those who seemed vanquished; where innumerable incidents arise unexpectedly which cannot possibly be foreseen or controlled by the commander's skill. So in this indecisive state of the battle, fortune, nor forgetting its usual power, did what neither men's courage nor force of arms had succeeded in doing.

The *stradiotti*, who had been sent to attack the wagons of the French, had begun to plunder them unopposed and were busy leading mules, horses and other equipment over to the other bank, when not only the other part of the *stradiotti* which was supposed to attack the French flank, but also those who had already entered the battle, saw their companions returning to camp laden with spoils. Fired with greed for gain, they turned to rob the wagons. Cavalry and infantry followed their example and abandoned the battle in large numbers for the same purpose. Therefore, as the Italians not only lacked their planned reinforcements but the number of combatants were diminishing through such disorder; and as Antonio da Montefeltro made no move because it was Ridolfo da Gonzaga's job to call him at the right moment – and Ridolfo was dead so no one called him – the French began to gain so much ground that the only thing still supporting the Italians, who were now visibly failing, was the courage of the Marquis. Fighting most bravely he still held the enemy attack, inspiring his men with his example and shouts of encouragement to prefer death to dishonor. But it was no longer possible for a few to resist many. The fight was thickening around them on all sides, many were dead and many wounded particularly in the Marquis' own company, and they were all forced to flee across the river. Because of the rains that had fallen that night, and which continued to fall with much hail and thunder while they were fighting, the river had risen so high that it was very hard to cross. The French pursued them vigorously to the river, concentrating with great fury on killing those who fled, without taking any prisoners or stopping for plunder or gain. Frequent cries were heard in the field: 'Comrades, remember Guinegate'. Guinegate is a place in Picardy near Thérouanne, where in the last years of the reign of Louis XI the French army, which had almost achieved victory in a battle against Maximilian, King of the Romans, fell into disorder when it started to plunder, and was put to flight.

But at the very moment when this part of the army was fighting with such courage and ferocity, the French vanguard, against which the Count of Gaiazzo sent part of his cavalry, moved into battle with such frightening violence, that the Italians, especially when they saw that they were not being followed by their own troops, fell into disarray almost of their own accord. And when some of their number had been killed – among them Giovanni Piccinino and Galeazzo da Coreggio – they returned in flight to the main squadron. The Marshal de Gié, however, seeing that besides the Count's squadron there was on the farther shore of the river another column of men-at-arms in battle order, would not allow his troops to pursue them. This was a decision which many, when it was later discussed, judged prudent; while many others who considered the effect more than the cause, regarded it as more cowardly than circumspect. For there is no doubt that if they had pursued them, the Count and his column would have turned tail, filling with such fear all the other troops on the other side of the river that it would have been virtually impossible to prevent them from running away. The Marquis of Mantua, fleeing from the other part of the army, crossed the river with part of his troops in as good order as he could manage and found these forces in such agitation that they were all thinking of saving themselves and their goods. The main road from Piacenza to Parma was already full of men, horses and wagons retreating toward Parma. His presence and authority put a stop in part to this tumult because he re-formed them and put some order into things. But the arrival of the Count of Pitigliano did much more; for amid all the confusion on both sides he had seized the opportunity to flee to the Italian camp, where he revived and strengthened their spirits by insistently assuring them that the enemy was in much greater alarm and confusion. Indeed it was almost universally claimed that if it had not been for his words, either then or the following night the whole army would have fled in terror.

The Italians had now retreated to their camp except for those who, driven by the confusion and tumult (as always happens in such circumstances) and frightened by the high waters of the river, had run away in different directions – many of them being found and slaughtered by the French scattered over the countryside. The King then went with his troops to join the vanguard which had not moved from its position, and there took counsel with his captains whether they should cross the river at once to attack the enemy in their camp. He was advised by Trivulzio and Cammillo Vitelli (whose company had been sent after the forces going on the Genoa campaign, while he had followed the King with a few cavalry to be present at the battle) to attack. Francesco Secco urged this course most strongly of all, pointing out that the road which could be seen in the distance was full of men and horses – which showed that either they were fleeing toward Parma or, having begun to flee, were now returning to their camp. Nevertheless it was not easy to cross the river. The troops who had either been fighting or had stood to arms in the field were so weary that on the advice of the French captains they decided to camp. They went to camp in the village of Medesano on the hill not much more than a mile from the place where they had fought. There they camped without any plan or order and with no little discomfort because many of their wagons had been looted by the enemy.

This was the battle fought between the Italians and the French on the River Taro, memorable because it was the first for a very long time which had been fought with killing and bloodshed in Italy.

> F. Guicciardini, *History of Italy*, trans. C. Grayson, (1964) New York, pp. 239f.

The third set-piece was the speech: the most popular in its own time, the least easy to appreciate now, when education no longer stresses rhetoric and historians find such conventions of invented speech dishonest. In fact speeches were quite a convenient literary device for the historian to explain what he thought the motives of his characters were.

Antonio Bonfini, 1427-1502, an Italian, was court historian to King Matthias Corvinus of Hungary, and author of a history of Hungary which he called 'decades' in imitation of Livy. Here is a speech which he puts into the mouth of his patron's father, János Hunyadi, addressing his troops before they fought the Turks. The beginning of a battle was a favourite place for humanist historians to insert speeches into their narrative.

> My loyal soldiers and good friends, now is the time for you to wipe out all stain of infamy, if you incurred any in that calamitous defeat of Varna. Now is the time for you to recover your reputa-

tion for loyalty and valour, and to avenge yourselves for so many wrongs and injuries received at the hands of these cursed Turks and unbelieving Mohammedans. If you wish to show yourselves as brave as usual, you must know that, having the right on our side, although we are much less numerous than the enemy, we will make him feel that in valour, spirits, and generosity we have the advantage. For the soldiers of the Turk fight for the benefit of another, and for the advancement of a man who will not be grateful for their efforts. Even if they are victorious, they can hope for no more than slavery for their whole lives, and the loss of their souls after death, because they have served the most powerful and detestable tyrant on earth. My friends and faithful companions, whether fortune follows you or turns her back on you, you are fighting for our kingdom, for the safety of your wives and children, for your temples and altars, for your homes, and in order to enjoy eternal happiness after death. This is what moves you to fight so fiercely: the knowledge that if you do not win, what happens to your goods, your wives and children, and to the whole realm happens by your own acts. You know well enough what the Turks' forces are worth, and ours too. The fortune of battles is uncertain, as was shown at the defeat of Varna. All the same, our ruin was not complete. The Turk would not have allowed us to escape had not his enormous losses left him without the strength or the means to pursue us. I must admit that although the Turk suffered heavier losses than we did, the dishonour was ours; by choosing to flee you we were responsible for your shame. But what is the use of lamenting? This defeat shows that God was angry and took vengeance for our breach of faith, for all those responsible for the breach lost their lives miserably there. We, however, who went with you in this war, are (thanks be to God) still living, preserved for the defence of Christendom and, above all, of Hungary, in order that it should not be exposed by our death to the tyrannical rage of the Turks . . .

Let us deliver Hungary from fear, in order that it may enjoy peace and live happily henceforward in a lasting tranquillity. My comrades, you must fight with all your strength, since necessity requires it, honour demands it, and our own interest advises it: for however fortune treats us, we cannot be otherwise than happy. If we are victorious, we have won the safety, peace and happiness of our country, and imperishable praise of ourselves: if we die, it is on the bed of honour and in a holy war that we leave this world, in order to enjoy a more happy life in the next. For this reason my friends, let us go and fight so well and bravely that whether we conquer or die, posterity will remember us with praise, and we will win the immortal crown or glory.

Antonio Bonfini,  *History o Hungary*,  3rd decade, book VII

As their use of set-pieces shows, Renaissance historians, or many of them at least, were enormously concerned about literary form. This concern extended to language: for example, historians were sometimes extremely worried about how to deal with place names and such modern inventions as cannon when writing in classical Latin. Leonardo Bruni declared that when he was wondering whether to write his history of the Florentine people,

> the sheer clumsiness of the names, scarcely capable of being rendered into elegant Latin . . . deterred me most strongly.

Lorenzo Valla was fiercely attacked by a brother-humanist because his history of the reign of Ferdinand of Aragon used words like 'bombarda', 'Mahometani' and 'parlamentum'.

Here again one sees the values of the humanists working against historical truth: they are trying to pretend that modern history is really just like ancient history, though Valla's sense of the history of language will not permit him to do this.

When the Venetian council of ten were deciding whom to appoint as state historian in 1516, they seem to have made their decision on literary grounds. They passed over Marino Sanudo, a learned man but no stylist, in favour of Andrea Navagero, whom they described as a man

> endowed with a remarkable knowledge of Greek and Latin literature, and with a style such that the opinion of the learned is that he has no equal in Italy or outside it.

Given these preoccupations of humanist historians, it is, perhaps, not surprising that the neighbour-subject of history was considered to be poetry. Giovanni Pontano, 1426-1503, makes this point in his dialogue *Actius*. By 'poetry' he means epic, in the style of Livy; given the importance of battle-scenes and speeches in both genres, the comparison is not as far-fetched as it might seem to the twentieth-century reader.

> The two subjects have much in common. They deal with events remote in space and time; they both describe the nature of places

and of peoples, where they live, what kind of manners, laws, and customs they have, with praise for their virtues and blame for their vices. Just as they both use the descriptive form, so they both make use of speeches, with which both poetry and history is greatly adorned, and they boast that something richer is drawn from them than from good authors. Besides this there are sudden accidents, diverse and unpredictable events, and contrary advice, matters which are more relevant to people's lives and problems than men themselves realise. An important function of poetry is to explain the intentions and actions of the gods. Similarly, history explains the anger of the gods, narrates prodigies, tells how the gods are placated by vows, by supplication, and by games in their honour, and interprets their oracles. Both history and poetry delight in amplifications, in digressions and in variety of matter; both try to move the passions; both follow the rule of decorum . . . But history is austere in language, poetry more voluptuous . . . in aim they differ completely, or very greatly, at any rate, since the purpose of history ought to be to tell the truth rather than to decorate it; whereas poetry does not satisfy nor do what is fitting for it unless it collects material from elsewhere, sometimes relating what is true or probable, sometimes relating what is altogether invented and not even plausible, in order to be the more marvelled at . . . the two subjects also differ in the order they follow, since history follows the order of the events themselves, whereas poetry often begins in the middle, or sometimes, at the end.

Giovanni Pontano, Actius, in Dialogues, ed.<br>C. Previtera, pp. 193-4

Humanist history was not just a matter of set-pieces, however. Historical writing was becoming more tightly organised; moving from the chronicle, of 'this year the Danes came' form, towards the monograph. Take the history of Florence by the famous humanist Leonardo Bruni. When he came to recent times, what he provided was a careful, detached, precise account of the war between Florence and the duke of Milan. He did not halt his narrative to analyse, but his views on the importance of economic factors, or the way in which men make political calculations, were present all the way through. One can see why B. L. Ullman called him, without qualification, 'the first modern historian.'

The Lord of Bologna [Giovanni Bentivoglio] was for the Florentines, but he feared the power of Milan, and so tried to stand in the middle, and refused to renew the alliance with the Florentines as they wished. However, being involved in war and having great anxieties, he was forced to ask the Florentines to aid him with horsemen. To show the world that he was on their side, the Florentines sent him not only the cavalry he had asked for, but their general Bernadone as well. So the war in the Bologna area was no longer a hidden one; and Bentivoglio's enemies had open aid from Giangaleazzo.

In Tuscany the war was not an open one, but the power of the duke of Milan grew every day, and it was clear that he would try to seize everything. Seeing this, the Florentines looked more and more to Ruprecht, the newly-elected emperor, hoping that if he came to Italy the power of Milan would wholly or partly vanish away – for there was bitter hatred between the two, and Ruprecht had declared publicly to cities and princes that Giangaleazzo had tried to poison him. With this hope in mind, the Florentines at length agreed with Ruprecht to pay him a large sum of money for coming to Italy. They promised him 2000 florins. It was agreed that he would receive half this sum before leaving home, and the balance when he arrived in Italy and invaded Giangaleazzo's territories. Ruprecht now made preparations to come to Italy, and the Florentines to pay him; each side sent frequent envoys to the other. Giovanni di Bicci was sent to pay over this huge sum of money; he was a prudent man and an honest one, with great credit among merchants. He carried out his assignment faithfully, and made the payment at Venice.

The rumour spread through Italy that great armies were making ready near the Rhine to come to Italy with the new emperor. Everyone was expectant. There was no less preparation in Milan – horses were got ready, money collected, towns and cities guarded, passes and rivers carefully watched . . .

The Florentines sent the emperor four more ambassadors, great nobles; Rinaldo Gianfigliazzi, Maso degli Albizzi, Filippo Corsini, Tommaso Sacchetti. They brought with them six hundred Italian horse in beautiful order, led by Sforza and Baldassare of Modena. They were well received by the emperor, but when they came to discuss what to do, they found him neither keen nor confident. He said that neither he nor the Florentines was strong enough to defeat Milan, and that it was necessary for the pope and Venice to join their league. He asked for so much money that it was obvious that he intended to do everything at the expense of the Florentines, nothing at his own. When the ambassadors realised this, they decided to send back to Florence Maso degli Albizzi and Andrea Vettori, (one of the earlier envoys to the emperor) to explain what they had seen and heard, for it was not convenient to do this in writing. When they returned and explained the situation to the council of citizens, everyone was dismayed. It seemed impossible to do what was asked, yet if the emperor departed it was clear what danger they would be in, for their enemy had increased in reputation and pride through his victory and would dare anything. Finally, after discussing the matter in council, it was decided to do everything they could to keep the emperor in Italy . . .

[However, the emperor left Italy; the Florentines were defeated and Bernadone captured; and Giangaleazzo took Bologna.]

When the Florentines heard that their army was defeated and their general captured, they were in great fear and trembling; but when they learned that Bologna was in the hands of the enemy, they trembled all the more, thinking that their enemies would appear at any moment. Having lost both their general and their army, everyone was in despair. If the enemy had hastened to follow up their victory, Florence would have been in a danger without any remedy. But they let the opportunity pass, whether from laziness or from internal dissensions. After many days had gone by and the enemy army had not arrived, the citizens gradually recovered their spirits and their strength . . .

While the city was intent on these matters, the rumour spread that duke Giangaleazzo was dead . . . At length the truth was discovered. Giangaleazzo had fallen ill not long after the fall of Bologna, and had finally died of his illness at Marignano, a castle in the Milanese. At first his death was concealed: when this was no longer possible, it was revealed and he was given a magnificent funeral. It was also learned that while he was ill Giangaleazzo had much wanted peace with the Florentines, and sent ambassadors to Venice to arrange it. He realised that he was leaving his young sons in the midst of great dangers, and so hastened to make peace before he died, and would actually have done so had he lived a little longer. From his sudden death followed very great changes. The men who had lost almost all hope of salvation were now confident in the extreme; the ones who had thought themselves on the brink of victory now lost any hope of resisting.

L. Bruni, *History of the Florentine People*, (1856-60) Florence, book XII

One may miss the vividness and spontaneity of a Froissart; but in their classical models, their attempt at objectivity, Renaissance historians are like Renaissance architects and artists.

These qualities continued to be appreciated after the taste for rhetorical set-pieces had declined. One can see the beginning of a re-action against them as early as Machiavelli and his *Florentine Histories*. Machiavelli inserts characters and speeches into his narrative, but he keeps them short. His 'anti-humanist' approach is still more obvious in a battle-scene, in his account of the battle of Anghiari, the battle which Leonardo had painted (above, p. 110). As Professor Felix Gilbert has remarked, Machiavelli describes the battle 'in the ornate manner required by humanist historical theory', but then deliberately spoils the effect with his remark that only one man was killed. Machiavelli does have an axe to grind here; he is against the employment of mer-cenaries, and wants to prove that it is useless to employ them. Modern historians estimate the casualties at Anghiari at several hundred. The passage is effective as a parody of humanist history none the less.

[The Milanese, under the mercenary leader Niccolò Piccinino, attacked the Florentines by crossing a bridge.]

The battle lasted for two hours, and sometimes Niccolò held the bridge, sometimes the Florentines. But although the battle on the bridge did not go either way, on both sides of it Niccolò was at a great disadvantage. For when his men crossed the bridge, they found the enemy unbroken, and the ground was level, so that they could manoeuvre, and those who were tired could be replaced by fresh troops; whereas when the Florentines crossed the bridge, Niccolò could not replace his men by fresh troops, being hindered by the ditches and embankments that ran along the roadside. The result was that Niccolò's men crossed the bridge many times, but they were always pushed back by the enemy, who were fresh. Then, when the Florentines had taken the bridge and were advancing along the road, Niccolò was unable to relieve his men in time, because of the fury of the advance and the obstacles on the ground. The result was that the men in front got mixed up with the men behind and threw them into disorder, so that the whole army was forced to turn tail and everyone fled towards Borgo without re-gard for anything else ... There was never a time when a war could be waged in enemy territory with less danger for the attackers than this. In such a great defeat as this one, and in a combat which lasted so long (from the 20th to the 24th hour),

E

only one man died; and he did not die of wounds or from some great blow, but fell off his horse and was trampled to death. Men used to fight with so little risk in those days. They were all on horseback and covered in armour, and if they surrendered they were sure not to be killed – so there was no reason for them to die. As long as they fought, their armour protected them, and when they could fight no more, surrender did.

N. Machiavelli, *Florentine History*, book V, chapter 33

By the time of Johann Sleidan, 1506-56, who wrote *Commentaries* on the reign of Charles V, the reaction against humanist history as too literary is turning into a movement. It is convenient to call this movement 'pragmatic' history, because its followers wanted to write something which was useful, and broke with the rhetorical tradition for this reason. Like humanist historians, they looked back to classical antiquity for a model, but to Polybius, not to Livy; for Polybius made fun of historians who invented speeches, calling them tragedians rather than historians; he too wanted history to be useful – *pragmatikos*. Sleidan set out to be the Polybius of the Reformation. His pages are full not of speeches but of documents. His aim was to be as objective as possible: to recite the facts (anticipating Ranke's famous phrase)

nakedly, simply, and in good faith, just as everything actually happened (*prout quaeque res acta fuit*).

It is difficult to give an impression of this book by a short extract; it makes its impact from negative virtues (not being rhetorical, not being prejudiced). Here is Sleidan's description of the origin of the Reformation.

At this time Martin Luther, of the Augustinian order, was at Wittenberg, a town in Saxony, on the river Elbe. He was disturbed by the sermons and the books of the preachers of indulgences, and seeing that people were believing what they were saying, he began to warn their customers to be prudent, and not to buy these goods at such a high price – for there were many better uses for their money. This happened in the year 1517. To make his labour more fruitful, at the end of October he wrote to Albert of Brandenberg, archbishop of Mainz, giving him to understand what these preachers of indulgences were teaching. He complained that the people firmly believed that if one bought these pardons, one could not fail to be saved; that there was no sin so great that these indulgences could not wipe it out; and that the souls tormented in the fire of purgatory were released from their sufferings and flew up to heaven as soon as the money was thrown into the collection-box. In addition, the said Luther declared that Christ had commanded the Gospel to be preached, and that the duty of bishops was to instruct the people. So he reminded the archbishop of his duty, and begged him to use his authority to prohibit these printed books and to command the preachers to teach the people something different, for fear that otherwise there would be some great conflict (*dissidium*), which could not fail to happen if they were not silenced. The reason for his writing to the said archbishop was that since he was also bishop of Magdeburg, he was responsible for these events. Together with these letters, Luther sent him 95 theses, which he had published at Wittenberg a short time before, for the purpose of holding a disputation. In these theses he discussed at length purgatory, true repentance, the duty of charity, and indulgences, and attacked the extravagant sermons of the preachers already mentioned. He did this, so it is said, simply to discover the truth. For he invited all who were interested to disputation, asking those who did not have the time to come in person to declare their opinion in writing. He declared that he did not want to affirm any conclusions, but simply to submit the whole question to the judgment of Holy Church. However, he declared that he would not accept the writings of St Thomas Aquinas and other such, except insofar as they agreed with the holy scriptures and the opinions of the Fathers.

> Johann Sleidan, *Commentaries*, (1555) Strasbourg, book I

Perhaps the greatest historian of the pragmatic school was fra Paolo Sarpi (above, p. 89) and its greatest work his masterpiece, the *History of the Council of Trent* (1619). His attitude to history, however, is more explicit elsewhere, in his books on the Uskoks (Christian refugees from the Turks in the Balkans, who became pirates on the Adriatic). He justifies his writing about such a 'low' subject, (thus breaking the humanist rule about preserving the dignity of history) in terms of its usefulness.

It is right for historians, whose aim is to record past events for posterity, to choose from them the most important and the most worthy of memory, and often to deal in a few words with everything that took place in whole decades. For the human mind is

limited and of small capacity; the reader will be confused by a
great number of facts, and he will learn nothing. Historians write
for men so distant from those whose actions form the subject of
the story that they do not feel either love or hate for them. So,
without displeasing the reader, they can take one piece of truth
and leave out another as they think best, according to what best
suits their aim of praising men or blaming them. I do not intend
to write in this manner, because my aim is to tell contemporary
readers about the causes and motives of the war provoked by the
insolence of the Uskoks, without having any regard for posterity.
This work will find many readers who have taken sides already,
who will think it unfair if even a small fact is omitted which might
support them; and those who are neutral, and read the book in
order to make up their minds which side is in the right, want an
exact and minute exposition of all the details, because, as the
lawyer well says, any tiny difference in the circumstances is
enough to alter the whole case. I should like this work of mine to
be read by everyone at present and as long as the disturbances last,
if only so that they know which side to pray for. I shall not advise
anyone to read it after it has pleased his divine majesty to put an
end to the troubles, because, although I have been most careful
to present a true and sincere narration, and to suspend my judgement, the reader will find that in other respects the laws of history
have not been obeyed, and will consider that the greater part of
the events narrated ought to be passed over in silence, since the
subject is such a low one. Should the book happen to fall into the
hands of a reader who is curious enough to browse through it, but
bored by the detail and the length of the narrative, I ask him to
forgive me, because my aim was not his pleasure or his profit, but
that of those who needed to be informed of every little detail.
From considering these events, everyone will be convinced that
if as people behaves insolently towards its neighbour, this must
always eventually lead to war, not only because the prudent
victim becomes tired of being victimised, but also because the
aggressor tires of meeting no resistance.

P. Sarpi, *Supplement to the History of the
Uskoks*, (1613), ed. G. and L. Cozzi, (1965)
Bari, pp. 73-4

Another pragmatic historian was Sarpi's English contemporary
William Camden, whose antiquarian researches have already been dis-

cussed (above, p. 31). Camden was a cautious man. He never quite openly rejected the myth of Brutus, though it seems clear that he did not believe in it. Similarly, he never quite rejects humanist history, while in practice moving away from it. In the preface to his *Annals of Queen Elizabeth* (1615) he declares that he will leave out speeches; and that (like Polybius) he believes explanation to be the great duty of the historian. At the same time, he refuses to look for hidden motives ('the unsearchable intents of princes') and defends the dignity of history ('to run through the most eminent actions, and not to dwell upon small ones'). As an official historian, he is careful not to follow truth too near the heels.

William Cecil, baron of Burghley, lord high treasurer of England (about sixteen years past) opened unto me (far from my thought) first some memorials of state of his own; afterwards, those of the kingdom; and from them willed me to compile a history of Queen Elizabeth's reign from the beginning . . . I sedulously volved and revolved characters of kings and peers, letters, consultations held at the council-table; I ran through the instructions and letters of ambassadors, and likewise the records and journals of parliaments, Acts and Statutes, and read over all proclamations . . . I have seen and observed much, and have from older men than myself, worthy of belief, (who were present when these were acted, and studious on both sides, in the division of religion) received them . . . The study of truth, as it hath been the only spur to prick me forward to the work; so it hath been my only scope. To detract from history is nothing else than to pluck out the eyes of a beautiful creature and, for a medicinable potion, to offer poison to the reader's understanding . . . Things manifest, I have not concealed; things doubtful, I have tenderly interpreted; the more abstruse, I have not been too inquisitive of; the unsearchable intents of princes (saith that prince of history) and what they out of reasons of state pretend, is not fit to enquire, and being doubtful, not to be explored. And with Halicarnasseus I am justly angry with the ignorant critics, who go about to know or find out more than is justly permitted. As to the rest, although I know that matters military and politic are the proper subjects of an historian, yet I neither could nor ought to omit ecclesiastical affairs (for betwixt religion and policy there can be no divorce). But seeing the writer of the ecclesiastical history may lawfully challenge these things as proper to himself, I have not touched at

them otherwise than with a light and cursory hand; whereas it is
the law and dignity of an historian to run through the most
eminent actions, and not to dwell upon small ones. I have not,
therefore, laboured in them . . . I have not omitted any circumstances by which not only the events of things, but their reasons
also and causes may be known; that of Polybius pleaseth me ex-
ceedingly. If you take out of history why, how, and to what end,
and what is done, and whether the actions answer the intents, that
that remains is rather a mocking than an instruction; and for the
present may please, but will never profit posterity . . . I have thrust
in no orations but such as were truly spoken; or those reduced to
fewer words: much less have I feigned any. I have seldom used
sentences [maxims] not beautified my discourse with those observations which the Greeks aptly call *epistaseis* [stoppages], my
intent being as it were insensibly to instruct the reader. I have
shunned digressions; I have used formal words; I have not
neglected descriptions of places, pedigrees or chronologies, following, as near as is possible, the order of the times.

> William Camden, *Annals*, (1615). Preface
> trans. Abraham Darcy; modernised spelling
> and punctuation and amended misprints

A last example of pragmatic history, and of the art of historical
narrative, is that of Jacques-Auguste de Thou, 1553-1617. He was a
friend of the great scholar Casaubon, and the correspondent of both
Camden and Sarpi. His most famous work is his *History of His Own Time*,
which covers the history of Europe from 1546 to 1607. His approach
to history tends to reduce religious motives to political ones, as Sarpi
does; de Thou was in fact a 'politique' and a councillor to Henri IV
before he became King. Like Davila, he blames the Guises rather than
the Protestants for the wars of religion; and in the passage quoted
below, he sees the war between Charles V and the Lutheran princes
(like Sleidan) basically in political terms. Like Pasquier and Bacon, he
is interested in cultural history, and inserts the obituary of Ronsard,
for example, into his narrative. The following passage is his comment on
Charles V's victory over Johann Friedrich of Saxony at Mühlberg in
1547.

> Such was the conclusion this year of the German war, the most
> memorable of any in that nation, either in our times or those of
> our ancestors, since the dissolution of the Roman empire; and I
> should not truly condemn those who would attribute the con-

clusion of it to the valour and prudence of the emperor. His very
enemies cannot deny that he gave the highest proof of heroic
bravery and an undaunted spirit at the camp before Ingolstadt;
where, being surrounded and almost overpowered by the
numerous and fresh army of the confederates, he not only be-
trayed not the least mark of fear, but diligently fortifying his camp,
encouraged his men by gallant speeches, and his own example.
The greater and the more imminent the danger, so much the more
alacrity he infused into them to surmount it, being himself both a
witness of their achievements and their leader. It was an instance
of noble courage in him, when a consultation was held about
breaking up the army and putting it into winter quarters, that he
chose to lie in the field with his men, covered only with skins, in
a very sharp winter, and thereby set an example to the soldiers of
soldierly patience. And it was an instance of no less prudence in
him to be forming an expedition so many years in such manner
that they against whom it was being prepared had not for a long
time the least suspicion of it; and at last to incite the Germans
against one another, drawing some into his party by playing on
their hopes, and others by working on their fears, so that he led
them on by mutual slaughter to promote their own destruction.
To these things, add the private animosities of the princes Albert
and John of the house of Brandenburg against the Landgrave of
Hesse, the ambition of duke Maurice, and his secret ill-will on that
account to John Frederick; all which the emperor with notable
art and cunning turned to his own service, and taking advantage of
their blind passions, hurried them to overlook the interest of the
religion which they professed and the liberty of Germany; to
employ their weapons against one another, which ought only to
have been drawn in defence of their country, and to open a way
for foreign soldiers to invade and subdue them. Nor was it the
least masterpiece of his policy, that passing a true judgement upon
the affairs of the confederates, he determined rather to keep off
from an engagement at first, than to come to a battle. He concluded
very justly from the nature of alliances and combinations of that
kind, that there could not be a lasting agreement between so many
cities and princes, who differed so greatly in their form of government. He also foresaw that where the power and authority of the
leaders were equal, no useful measures could be taken, concealed,
or executed at the proper moment. As the principal force of the
confederacy lay in the cities, by whose money the soldiers were to

be maintained, and the war supported, he knew the temper of the citizens to be impatient of all delays, and that if the war were carried on at any length, they would immediately impute any instance of slowness (which is often necessary), to the ambition or cunning of their generals, and at last, growing weary of the war, would refuse their quotas and withdraw from the confederacy.

De Thou, *History of His Own Time*, (1604), adapted from the trans. by Bernard Wilson, (1729) London, pp. 199–200

# VI

# CLASSICAL AND EARLY CHRISTIAN HISTORICAL THOUGHT

Renaissance historians saw themselves as returning to the ancient methods of writing history, as modern Livys or Sallusts. But did they? Did the Greeks and Romans have the sense of history, as it has been defined throughout this book?

## 1 Historical Narrative

There is no doubt that, so far as literary form is concerned, Renaissance historians differ from medieval ones because they model themselves on the ancients. The set-pieces of humanist history have their parallels, or rather their models, in Thucydides, *c.* 460–*c.* 399 B.C. Livy 59 B.C.–17 A.D. and others. This is true of the character and of the speech.

Livy's character of Hannibal is a famous one. Guicciardini seems to have borrowed some traits from it for his Alexander (above, p. 108).

Hannibal was sent to Spain, where he was no sooner come than he won the favour of the entire army. The old soldiers thought that Hamilcar was restored to them as he had been in his youth; they beheld the same lively expression and piercing eye, the same cast of countenance and features. But he soon brought it to pass that his likeness to his father was the least consideration in gaining him support. Never was the same nature more adaptable to things the most diverse – obedience and command. And so one could not readily have told whether he was dearer to the general or the army. When any bold or difficult deed was to be done, there was no one whom Hasdrubal liked better to entrust with it, nor did any other leader inspire his men with greater confidence or daring. To reckless courage in incurring dangers he united the greatest judgement when in the midst of them. No toil could exhaust his body or overcome his spirit. Of heat and cold he was equally tolerant. His consumption of meat and drink was determined by natural desire, not by pleasure. His times of waking and sleeping were not marked off by day or night: what time remained when his work was done he gave to sleep, which he did not court with a soft bed or stillness, but was seen repeatedly by many lying on the ground wrapped in a common soldier's cloak amongst the sentinels and outguards. His dress was in no way superior to that of his fellows, but his arms and horses were conspicuous. Both of horsemen and foot-soldiers he was undoubtedly the first – foremost to enter battle, and last to leave it when the fighting had begun. These admirable qualities of the man were equalled by his monstrous vices: his cruelty was inhuman, his perfidy worse than Punic; he had no regard for truth, and none for sanctity, no fear of the gods, no reverence for an oath, no religious scruple. With this endowment of good and evil traits he served for the space of three years under Hasdrubal, omitting nothing that should be done or seen by one who was to become a great commander.

> Livy, XXI.4, trans. B. O. Foster for the Loeb
> edition, (1957) London and Cambridge Mass.,
> .pp. 9–13

One of the masters of the historical speech is Thucydides, who incidentally makes it clear, as his Renaissance imitators usually do not, that the actual words are his own invention, even though they express what he believed was called for by each situation. As a parallel to the speech from Bonfinio (above, p. 117) I have chosen another battle situation. The speech serves the function in the narrative of encouraging the troops, and at the same time serves the function for the reader of suggesting the issues at stake and the motives of the leaders. The speaker here is Phormio, commander of the Athenian naval forces, who are about to fight the Peloponnesians.

I see, my men, that you are alarmed by the enemy's numbers, and I have called this meeting because I do not want you to be frightened when there is no occasion to be so. First of all, the reason why they have equipped this great number of ships and are not meeting on even terms is that they have been defeated once already and do not even think themselves that they are a match for us. The thing which gives them most confidence in facing us is that they imagine themselves to have a kind of monopoly in being brave, yet this comforting belief is based simply on their experience in land fighting, in which they have won many victories. They think that this experience of theirs will be equally valuable on the sea; but here, if there is anything in their argument, the advantage will be on our side. They are certainly no braver than we are, and as for feeling confident, both they and we have that feeling with regard to the element where we have the greater experience . . . When one side is in superior numbers, as our enemy is, it makes its attack relying more on force than on resolution. But if the other side, far weaker in material resources, takes up the challenge, when there is no compulsion to do so, it means that that side has something in mind to fall back upon which is very great indeed. This is what our enemies are reckoning on, and they are more frightened by the unexpectedness of our action than they would be if we were meeting them on reasonably equal terms. Great forces before now have been defeated by small ones because of lack of skill and sometimes because of lack of daring. We are deficient in neither of these qualities.

Now as for the battle, if I can help it, I shall not fight it in the gulf, nor shall I sail into the gulf. I fully realise that lack of sea room is a disadvantage for a small, experienced, and fast squadron fighting with a lot of badly managed ships. One cannot sail up in the proper way to make an attack by ramming, unless one has a good long view of the enemy ahead, nor can one back away at the right moment if one is hard pressed oneself; it is impossible also to sail through the enemy's line and then wheel back on him – which are the right tactics for the fleet which has the superior seamanship.

> Thucydides, book II, trans. R. Warner, (1954)
> London, p. 151

The reader will have noticed one significant difference between this speech and the one in Bonfinio: Thucydides does not confine his general to moral exhortation, but lets him discuss technical details. But then Thucydides had military experience, Bonfinio had not.

Again, the idea of the dignity of history is not a Renaissance invention, but may be found in Roman writers; in Tacitus, c. 55-120 A.D. for example. Sir Ronald Syme has noted how Tacitus suppressed details that he found undignified, like the fact that Sulpicius Galba was bald, or the circumstances surrounding the death of Vitellius. Suetonius had no such scruples. Thus Suetonius describes Vitellius as accompanied by his pastry-cook and his chef; Tacitus has 'the meanest of his slaves'. Suetonius describes Vitellius hiding in the porter's lodge; Tacitus has 'an unseemly hiding-place'. Suetonius says that the people called Vitellius 'Greedy-guts'; Tacitus only mentions 'insults'.

If humanist history owes its literary form to the ancients, so does the pragmatic reaction against it. Camden, declaring his aims in the preface to his *Annals* (above, p. 127), was echoing Polybius *c.* 200-*c.* 118 B.C., whose attack on Timaeus of Tauromenium was a manifesto for his new kind of history, with the speeches left out and the explanations put in.

> By way of convincing those who might still wish to defend Timaeus, I may perhaps discuss his method especially as regards the speeches and exhortations in his work ... he has recorded accurately neither what was said nor the manner in which it was spoken; instead, he uses as his model what he thinks ought to have been said, and then recounts the speeches delivered and the accompanying circumstances in the manner of someone trying to discuss a set theme in a school of rhetoric, as if he were giving a display of his powers of eloquence rather than an account of what was actually said ...
>
> The special function of history consists, first in ascertaining as nearly as possible the words actually spoken and second, in discovering the cause of the failure or success of whatever was done or said; for if only the bare facts about an event are narrated, it may provide pleasant reading but cannot be of any real benefit, while if the cause of the event is duly added the study of history becomes fruitful.
>
> Polybius, *Histories*, book XII, 25, trans. M. Chambers, (1966) New York, pp. 279-83

It should perhaps be added that Polybius believed that only men with military experience should write military history, and that only men with political experience should write political history; criteria which would have excluded Camden, who was a schoolmaster and antiquary, from writing the *Annals* at all.

## 2 Historical Explanation

This last passage from Polybius also shows that the interest in historical explanation was very strong in the ancient world. Machiavelli and Guicciardini, in their discussions of the power of *Fortuna*, may well have been thinking of Polybius, and his equivalent discussions of the power of *Tyche*. Thucydides was influenced by Hippocratic medicine and believed that the historian, like the physician, could produce a diagnosis. One of the most famous passages in his history is his description of the symptoms, causes and effects of revolution; a passage which might usefully be compared with the analysis of the English civil war by his translator, Thomas Hobbes (above p. 95)

> In times of peace and prosperity cities and individuals alike follow higher standards, because they are not forced into a situation where they have to do what they do not want to do. But war is a stern teacher; in depriving them of the power of easily satisfying their daily wants, it brings most people's minds down to the level of their actual circumstances.
>
> So revolutions broke out in city after city, and in places where the revolutions occurred late the knoweldge of what had happened previously in other places caused still new extravagances of revolutionary zeal, expressed by an elaboration in the methods of seizing power and by unheard-of atrocities in revenge. To fit in with the change of events, words, too, had to change their usual meanings. What used to be described as a thoughtless act of aggression was now regarded as the courage one would expect to find in a party member; to think of the future and wait was merely another way of saying one was a coward; any idea of moderation was just an attempt to disguise one's unmanly character; ability to understand a question from all sides meant that one was totally unfitted for action ... Love of power, operating through greed and through personal ambition, was the cause of all these evils. To this must be added the violent fanaticism which came into play once the stuggle had broken out.
>
> Thucydides, book III, trans. R. Warner, (1954) London, p. 208

Among Roman historians, Tacitus is perhaps the most interested in explanation; early in his *Histories* he declares that he wants to present not only what happened (*casus, eventus*) but why (*ratio, causae*). Like Thucydides, he is fascinated by collective psychology, and by the true motives behind official masks. Machiavelli and Guicciardini, Sarpi and Davila, Clarendon and Hobbes, great as they are, never surpassed their classical masters in the art of historical explanation.

The cyclical interpretation of history current at the Renaissance has its classical parallels – and sources. Polybius, for example, believed in cycles.

> In the period when they were about to enter on the Hannibalic war, the Carthaginian constitution had become worse and the Roman better. Every physical body, every constitution, and every enterprise has a certain kind of growth according to nature, and following that its climax, and afterward its decay.
>
> Polybius, book VI, p. 51, trans. M. Chambers,
> (1966) New York, p. 260

In Roman times, the Stoics believed in a cyclical view of history; in some cases, at least, in complete repetition – the eternal recurrence of exactly the same men and events. Origen 186-253, the father of the Church, writing against Celsum, attributed such a view of history to him and attacked it.

> If this is true, free will is destroyed. For if 'it is inevitable that in the period of mortal life according to the determined cycles the same things always have happened, are now happening, and will happen', it is obviously inevitable that Socrates will always be a philosopher, and be accused of introducing new deities and corrupting the youth; Anytus and Meletus will always be accusing him, and the council on the Areopagus will vote for his condemnation to death by hemlock . . . The reply to this assumption of Celsus will be that . . . it is inevitable according to the determined cycles that Moses will always come out of Egypt with the people of the Jews; Jesus will again come to visit this life and will do the same things that he has done, not just once but an infinite number of times according to the cycles. Furthermore, the same people will be Christians in the determined cycles, and again Celsus will write his book, though he has written it before an infinite number of times.
>
> Origen, *Against Celsus*, IV.67, trans. H. Chadwick, (1953) Cambridge

## 3  Historical Evidence

Polybius's attack on Timaeus, and Thucydides' apology for inventing speeches are reminders, if reminders are needed, that at least some historians in antiquity were keenly aware of the need to base their statements upon good evidence. An interesting example of Greek historical criticism at work is Herodotus's handling of Homer as a historical source for the Trojan War. When he was in Memphis, Herodotus *c.* 485-425 B.C., visited a temple dedicated to Aphrodite the Stranger, and he asked the priests there about Helen of Troy. They told him that Paris and Helen had visited Memphis, then ruled by a certain Proteus. Herodotus then compared different versions of the Trojan story and criticised them on the grounds of inherent plausibility.

This was the account I had from the priests about the arrival of Helen at Proteus' court. I think Homer was familiar with the story; for though he rejected it as less suitable for epic poetry than the one he actually used, he left indications that it was not unknown to him . . . I asked the priests if the Greek story of what happened at Troy had any truth in it, and they gave me in reply some information which they claimed to have had direct from Menelaus himself. This was, that after the abduction of Helen, the Greeks sent a strong force to the Troad in support of Menelaus' cause, and as soon as the men had landed and established themselves on Trojan soil, ambassadors, of whom Menelaus was one, were dispatched to Troy. They were received within the walls of the town, and demanded the restoration of Helen together with the treasure which Paris had stolen, and also satisfaction for the injuries they had received. The Trojans, however, gave them the answer which they always stuck to afterwards – sometimes even swearing to the truth of it; namely, that neither Helen nor the treasure was in their possession, but both were in Egypt, and there was no justice in trying to force them to give satisfaction for property which was being detained by the Egyptian king Proteus. The Greeks, supposing this to be a merely frivolous answer, laid siege to the town, and persisted until it fell; but no Helen was found, and they were still told the same story, until at last they believed it and sent Menelaus to visit Proteus in Egypt. He sailed up the river to Memphis, and when he had given a true account of all that had happened, he was most hospitably entertained and Helen, none the worse for her adventures, was restored to him with all the rest of his property . . . This, then, is the version the Egyptian priests gave me of the story of Helen, and I am inclined to accept it for the following reason: had Helen really been in Troy, she would have been handed over to the Greeks with or without Paris' consent;

for I cannot believe that either Priam or any other kinsman of his was mad enough to be willing to risk his own and his children's lives and the safety of the city, simply to let Paris continue to live as Helen's husband.

> Herodotus, book II, trans. A. de Sélincourt,
> (1954) London, pp. 144-6

It is interesting to compare this passage with the beginning of the history of Thucydides, which discusses the same source, Homer; is equally critical; but asks different questions, about exact numbers and logistic problems. He suggests that Agamemnon's force was smaller than armies were in Thucydides' time, and explains this fact by lack of money and lack of supplies. He questions Homer's figures, which 'since he was a poet, were probably exaggerated'.

Finally, it is worth mentioning that in late classical times, the neoplatonist Porphyry, 233-304?, treated the Bible as a historical document, and checked its statements against other sources, such as Philo of Byblos.

# 4   The Sense of Anachronism

Did the Greeks and Romans lack the sense of anachronism? The customary opinion is that they did; that in this respect, the Renaissance sense of history was something quite new. The Greeks believed that only what was unchanging could be known. They believed that human nature was always the same; that the past tended to repeat itself. This was the value of the study of the past for Thucydides and for Polybius; it means that they were closer to what we call the social sciences than to what we call history. They did not see history in terms of different periods, each with its own characteristics. It is true that the poet Hesiod (seventh century B.C.) spoke of four ages of man – gold, silver, bronze and iron – but it is significant that he used the term 'race' (*genos*) for each one, and suggested that Zeus created them separately, not that they developed out of one another. It is tempting to see the idea of transition from a bronze age to an iron age as an oral tradition which correctly represents the facts of prehistory; but what is significant in this context is that Hesiod does not have the concepts to see this transition in terms of 'development'. Again, Aeschylus, 525-456 B.C., in his play *Prometheus* suggested that before his hero's time, men had no architecture, no ships, no medicine, and so on. But this is explanatory myth rather than history; there is no sense of development here. More of an exception is Herodotus, who wrote that

> it was only – if I may so put it – the day before yesterday that the Greeks came to know the origin and form of the various Gods,

and pointed out that the names of the gods came to Greece from Egypt. It is not surprising, then, that Polydore Vergil, writing about the history of religion (above, p. 39) made considerable use of Herodotus; Herodotus was aware that religion had a history. But this awareness was unusual in his time

It is in the later classical period that something more like the Renaissance sense of anachronism can be found. Late Hellenistic art (for example, the art of Athens in the late second century B.C.) was archaistic; it imitated the classical style, just as Renaissance art did. Some of the great Roman writers show an interest in the remote past and an awareness of change or development. Varro (116-27 B.C.) is an example. He wrote a book, now lost, except for some fragments, called the *Divine and Human Antiquities*. St Augustine described the book in his *City of God*, remarking that Varro dealt with such subjects as the history of priests, temples, festivals and rites. The parallel with a Polydore Vergil or a Biondo is obvious. Varro may be thought of as the first antiquarian, for he has the key idea of antiquarianism, 'the idea of a civilisation recovered by systematic collection of all the relics of the past' (Momigliano), an idea which was lost during the Middle Ages and recovered at the Renaissance. Varro was also interested in chronology; he secured agreement among his contemporaries on the year of the foundation of Rome, as a basis for calculating other dates.

Cicero, 106-43 B.C. has an awareness of development over time. He can describe certain words as being obsolete (*obsoletus*) He talks about eloquence being born and growing to maturity; starting in Greece, but later than other arts, then moving to Rome, where it took some time for orators to reach the Greek level. This discussion of oratory was of help to Vasari in his descriptions of the progress of Renaissance art.

Lucretius, *c.* 94-55 B.C. in his poem *On the Nature of Things*, has a remarkable and eloquent evocation of the life of primitive man which is one of the best illustrations of the Roman sense of the past. It is in the tradition of Hesiod and Aeschylus, but the gods are left out, leaving instead a sense of historical evolution, 'as time went by'.

The human beings that peopled these fields were far tougher than the men of today, as became the offspring of tough earth. They were built on a framework of bigger and solider bones, fastened through their flesh to stout sinews. They were relatively insensitive to heat and cold, to unaccustomed diet and bodily ailments in general. Through many decades of the sun's cyclic course they lived out their lives in the fashion of wild beasts roaming at large. No one spent his strength in guiding the curved plough. No one knew how to cleave the earth with iron, or to plant young saplings in the soil or lop the old branches from tall trees with pruning hooks ... They did not know as yet how to enlist the aid of fire, or to make use of skins, or to clothe their bodies with trophies of the chase. They lived in thickets and hillside caves and forests and stowed their rugged limbs among bushes when driven to seek shelter from the lash of wind and rain.

They could have no thought of the common good, no notion of the mutual restraint of morals and laws. The individual, taught only to live and fend for himself, carried off on his own account such prey as fortune brought him ...

As time went by, men began to build huts and to use skins and fire. Male and female learnt to live together in a stable union and to watch over their joint progeny. Then it was that humanity first began to mellow. Thanks to fire, their chilly bodies could no longer so easily endure the cold under the canopy of heaven. Venus subdued brute strength. Children by their wheedling easily broke down their parents' stubborn temper. Then neighbours began to form mutual alliances, wishing neither to do nor to suffer violence among themselves ...

As time went by, men learnt to change their old way of life by means of fire and other new inventions, instructed by those of outstanding ability and mental energy. Kings began to found cities and establish citadels for their own safeguard and refuge. They parcelled out cattle and lands, giving to each according to his looks, his strength and his ability; for good looks were highly prized and strength counted for much. Later came the invention of property and the discovery of gold, which speedily robbed the strong and the handsome of their preeminence ...

The art of mounting armed on horseback, guiding the steed with reins and keeping the right hand free for action, came earlier than braving the hazards of war in a two-horsed chariot ... As to costume, plaited clothes came before woven ones. Woven fabrics came after iron, because iron is needed for making a loom.

Lucretius, *On the Nature of Things*, trans. R. Latham, (1951) London, book V, pp. 199-213

This account of technological and social change is more modern than anything written at the Renaissance.

A generation later than Lucretius, Vergil, 70-19 B.C. is another poet with a sense of the past. This awareness of change is built into the *Aeneid*. Of course, there is a sense in which the poem is unhistorical; Vergil projects onto the remote past some features of the Rome of his own day. But he does this consciously, as a means of suggesting that his Rome has developed out of that primitive Rome and is linked to it. Vergil's characters, unlike those of Homer, have themselves a sense of the past and of the future. Like Petrarch's *Africa*, which imitated it, the Aeneid is in some sense a 'historical novel'.

Again, Horace, 65-8 B.C. shows an awareness of change in his *Art of Poetry*. He knows that costume changes, and refers to the earlier Romans as the 'girdled Cethegi' (*cinctuti Cethegi*) because some two hundred years before, Romans like M. Cornelius Cethegus wore the *cinctus* (a girdle or loincloth) under their togas. He is aware that language changes too, and compares the life of words to that of human beings; old ones die, and newly-born ones thrive. This passage from the *Art of Poetry* is the source of Chaucer's reflections about changing words and customs (above, p. 39). Thus the sense of history in one age stimulated the sense of history in another.

The lack of the sense of historical perspective in ancient Greece has often been emphasised. It is argued that modern historical thought arose from the fusion of Greek thought, with its emphasis on rational explanation, and Hebrew thought, with its emphasis on a dynamic, linear interpretation of history. However, what I should like to stress is the fact, relatively neglected, that the Romans did have the sense of historical perspective that the Greeks lacked; and that the Jews did not have it. Their linear interpretation of history was a metaphysical one – they saw the history of Israel as the fulfilment of a promise made by God – which did not involve any empirical sense of anachronism or change as I have defined it throughout this essay. In this respect, medieval historians followed the Jews: Renaissance historians followed the Romans.

# VII

# HISTORY AND SOCIETY

## 1 From the Renaissance to the Nineteenth Century

I hope that this essay has not given the impression that all the great advances in historical thinking took place between Petrarch and Spinoza, important as this period was. To correct this possible impression, it may be a good idea to give a thumb-nail sketch of later developments.

The late seventeenth century was more of an age of historical scholarship than of historical writing. Jean Mabillon's *On Diplomatic*, (1681) was the codification of rules for deciding the authenticity of documents which had been discovered by Petrarch, Valla, and their successors. Du Cange published in 1688 a dictionary of late classical and medieval Latin which became an indispensable reference book. It too was built on a Renaissance discovery; that language changed over time.

In the eighteenth century came the rise of social history, or 'civil history', as it was called by its pioneer, the Neapolitan Giannone, 1676-1748. It was then that – for the first time – historians wrote about trade and taste; law and literature; morals and music. Chapters of Gibbon, Hume, and Robertson are devoted to these topics. Voltaire not only wrote chapters of this kind in his *Age of Louis XIV*, but devoted a whole book to cultural and social history – his *Essay on Manners* of 1769. Historical explanations came to be given more in social, less in individual terms. For example, the idea of balance became part of the historian's explanatory equipment; Gibbon saw the decline of the Roman Empire as 'the natural and inevitable defect of immoderate greatness'. Marx's economic interpretation of history was built on eighteenth-century foundations. At the same time, historians tended to assume that human nature is always essentially the same, thus giving up the Renaissance interest in change. The Enlightenment ideal was that of the 'philosophical historian', and the philosophical spirit, as the eighteenth century defined it (we would use the term 'scientific'), consisted above all in the gift for seeing the particular as an example of the general; for showing that the historical events under consideration conformed to general laws. As Hume put it, in his essay on the study of history,

> The chief use of history is to discover the constant and universal principles of human nature . . . records of wars, intrigues, factions and revolutions are so many collections of experiments by which the politician or moral philosopher fixes the principles of his science.

Such an attitude is like that of a modern sociologist or political scientist. It is in the tradition of Thucydides and Machiavelli. But it is incompatible with a sense of historical perspective. It is as if historians could not at the same time be conscious of what societies and individuals have in common and of what makes them different; the realm of the social was conquered at the expense of the loss of the chronological.

The reaction against this 'philosophical' way of thinking came towards the end of the eighteenth century, and was linked to the rise of the Romantic movement. One of the essential differences between Enlightenment and Romantic thought was the difference between their images of man. The Romantics asserted that there were no 'constant and universal principles of human nature'; on the contrary, human nature differed for different individuals, nations, or periods. This point was made emphatically by J. G. Herder, 1744-1803, in his *Outlines for a Philosophy of the History of Man*, 1784-91. He was fascinated by the unfamiliar and the primitive and thought that the historian could learn to understand it through 'empathy' (*Einfühlung*). Similarly, the Danish historian B. G. Niebuhr, 1776-1831, criticised Montesquieu for having treated ancient Romans as if they were eighteenth-century Frenchmen. He thought it the historian's task to understand the 'otherness' of the past. In his own writings, he emphasised the primitive aspects of ancient Rome.

And so, at the beginning of the nineteenth century, historians rediscovered the sense of anachronism, which became more acute for some of them than it had been for any Renaissance historian. And not only for them, but for educated men in general. It was at this time that the historical drama and the historical novel made their appearance; that is, plays and novels where an attempt is made not to modernise the psychology of the characters. This new movement starts with Goethe, 1749-1832, who was a friend of Herder's when they were both in their twenties and was encouraged by him to take a subject from German history. Goethe's play *Götz von Berlichingen* (1771) is set in sixteenth-century Germany. Scott, 1771-1832, who was much impressed by *Götz*, was the creator of the historical novel; *Ivanhoe* (1820) and *Quentin Durward* (1823) are famous examples. Scott was in his turn an inspiration to the Italian Manzoni, 1785-1873, whose masterpiece *The Betrothed* (1825-7) was set in seventeenth-century Milan. At the same time, an increased awareness of anachronism in costume was developing. In England, the 1823 production of Shakespeare's *King John* at Drury Lane is said to have been the first to attempt correct medieval costumes.

The nineteenth-century discovery of the past was curiously like the Renaissance discovery, of which – after a gap – it was a continuation, an intensification. Philology again played a crucial role, with Niebuhr in the place of Valla. A historical school of law came into existence once again, with Savigny, 1779-1861, in the place of Alciati and Cujas. Savigny, who taught at Berlin, saw law as a gradual development or growth like language; his greatest pupil was the philologist Jakob Grimm. The approach to the Bible as a historical document carried on from where Spinoza had left off with the work of Eichhorn, another friend of Herder's and the author of a famous *Introduction to the Old Testament*, 1780-83. And just as Renaissance architecture imitated classical antiquity, so the early nineteenth century was the age of the Gothic Revival.

It is not only in its sense of historical perspective that the early nineteenth century is like the Renaissance. The criticism of sources went through another revolution, a continuation and intensification of the earlier one. As Lord Acton put it later in the century, historians in his time were at the beginning of 'the documentary age, which will tend to make history independent of historians'. Acton pointed to Ranke, 1795-1886, as 'the real originator of the heroic study of records'. It was he, for example, who first made serious use of the reports of the Venetian ambassadors as a historical source, and hoped by the use of such evidence to write history 'as it actually happened' (*wie es eigentlich gewesen ist*). The formula, and to a lesser extent the practice, had been anticipated by Sleidan in the sixteenth century (above, p. 124), but now the trend went further. There was a general displacement of interest from narrative sources, or 'chronicles', to documentary sources, or 'records', on the grounds that records were more reliable.

At the same time, non-literary evidence received more attention than ever before, and this led to the discovery of 'prehistory' – the period before the invention of writing. Thomsen, the curator of the Danish National Museum of Antiquities, classified his collection into three ages; the stone age, the bronze age and the iron age. He published his catalogue with this classification in 1836. The result was to destroy the idea of the six thousand year world, common to St. Augustine and to Renaissance writers, and to substitute a much longer history of man. This method of classification was one important difference between modern archaeology and Renaissance antiquarianism, out of which it developed. Another important difference was that in the mid-nineteenth century, excavation became a scientific technique, instead of a way of finding objects for collections of antiquities. Pioneers of the new technique were Schliemann, 1822-90, who discovered Troy, cutting through a mound and distinguishing seven different strata occupied at different periods; and Pitt-Rivers, 1827-1900, who excavated barrows on his own estates in England, and was careful to record the position of every object he found, since the position of the object was as much historical evidence as the object itself.

## 2 A Comparative Approach

The development of the sense of history, as I have defined it throughout this essay, took place within the Western tradition, from Greece to Rome, from Renaissance to Romanticism. Is it confined to the Western tradition? To a very large extent it is. The one non-Western civilisation in which the writing of history was considered an important activity was China, from the Han dynasty (from 206 B.C.) onwards. But Chinese historians in general lacked the sense of historical perspective, awareness of evidence, and interest in explanation. Let me briefly try to justify these generalisations.

First, the lack of historical perspective. Some isolated passages can be found which contradict this generalisation, but there are not many of them. One of the most famous comes from the writings of Chuang Tzu, who flourished in the fourth century B.C.

> Our time and that of the former kings are as different as land from water; the empire of Chou over which they ruled and this land of Lu are as different as boat from chariot. Your master tries to treat the Lu of today as though it were the Chou of long ago. This is like pushing a boat over dry land.
>
> Chuang Tzu, trans. A. Waley in his *Three Ways of Thought in Ancient China*, (1956 edition) New York, p. 19

The phrase 'your master' refers to Confucius. The suggestion is that Confucius respected tradition too much and so lacked historical perspective. Chuang Tzu was a Taoist and anti-Confucian; but it was Confucius who triumphed. Had Taoism won, it is possible that both history and science would have developed earlier and further than they in fact did.

Some two thousand years later, Wang Ch'uan-shan, 1619-92, showed a sense of anachronism, of the inapplicability of ancient institutions to modern times, much like that of Hotman (above, p. 34)

> The ancient institutions were designed to govern the ancient world, and cannot be applied to the present day. Therefore the wise man does not try to set up detailed systems, . . . situations change, conditions are different . . . when it comes to questions of particular facts and laws, then one must follow the times and try to determine what is fitting in each case.
>
> Wang Ch'uan-shan, trans. in E. Balazs, *Political Theory and Administrative Reality*, (1965) London, p. 42

Wang Ch'uan-shan was also unable to make headway against Confucian orthodoxy. The sense of anachronism was able to develop in one area alone – in art. Chinese painters often imitated the style of masters who flourished centuries earlier.

Again, Chinese historians generally lacked any sharp awareness of the nature and limitations of historical evidence. Just as they lacked a sense of the past because they believed in tradition, so, one might argue, they lacked a sense of evidence because they had too many records, not too few. The traditional primary sources for political events were the 'diaries of activity and repose' of the emperor, diaries which went back to Han times at least. In T'ang times, 618-907 A.D., there were diarists of the right and left who stood each side of the imperial throne; the left recorded his actions, the right his words. At the end of each season, the diaries were submitted to the History Department, *shih-kuan*. Reports from the provinces and from government departments were also submitted. However, the histories that were written exhibited the defects as well as the merits of this 'bureaucratisation'. The official documents were copied but not criticised. The official version of the past was simply accepted. The hesitations of two thinkers bold enough to challenge this system are vivid illustrations of its strength.

Liu Chih-chi, A.D. 661-721, in a passage which one wishes could have been brought to the notice of some Renaissance humanists, objected to tampering with the actual words of historical figures – for example, the current practice of putting classical allusions into the mouths of barbarian rulers.

> If things are all to be recorded without error the words must be close to the actual ones, so that one may almost dwell with the men of the past. Why should one be content with their chaff and husks?
>
> *Historians of China and Japan*, ed. Beasley and Pulleyblank and trans. E. G. Pulleyblank, (1961) London, p. 147

But Liu was embarrassed by his own desire for innovation, as he admits.

> I feared that . . . I would startle vulgar opinion and be blamed by my contemporaries, receiving no thanks for my trouble. Whenever I took my writing-brush in hand, I would sigh irresolutely . . .
>
> (*ibid.* p. 138)

Ssu-ma Kuang (eleventh century) was more critical still. He turned his attention not, like Liu, to what goes wrong when the historian has the records and is writing history, but to what has already gone wrong in the records before they reach him; the problem of resolving discrepancies. He wrote a famous letter to his research assistant Fan Tsu-yü about problems of the history of the T'ang dynasty.

> If the accounts contain discrepancies as to dating or facts, then I request that you choose one version for which the evidence is clear, or which in the nature of the case seems to be closest to the truth, and write it into the main text. The result should be placed below in a note and in addition you should set forth there the reasons for accepting one version and rejecting the others . . . Veritable Records [*shih-lu*, a particular type of official histories] and Official Histories are not necessarily always to be relied upon, miscellaneous histories and anecdotes are not necessarily without foundation. Make your choice by your own scrutiny.
>
> (*ibid.* p. 162)

The third criterion of the Western sense of history is interest in explanation. This too was generally lacking in Chinese historians, but not in Ssu-ma Ch'ien, 145-c. 90 B.C. He described his work and plans in another famous letter, to Jen An.

> I studied the events of history and set them down in significant order; I have written 130 chapters in which appears the record of the past – its periods of greatness and decline, of achievement and failure. Further it was my hope, by a thorough comprehension of the workings of affairs divine and human, and a knowledge of historical process, to create a philosophy of my own.
>
> > *Anthology of Chinese Literature*, ed. C. Birch and trans. J. R. Hightower, (1965) London p. 126

However, disaster overtook Ssu-ma Ch'ien before he could achieve his aims, and his successors lowered their sights. Chinese historians tended to restrict themselves to a bare narrative of facts. Where explanations were offered at all, they were usually stereotyped ones. A favourite idea was that of the dynastic cycle – dynasties were believed to be founded by virtuous heroic men and to come to an end under weak or wicked men, and these characteristics of individuals were offered as explanations of the dynastic changes. In fact this is myth, not history; the reasoning is circular; if a man is the last ruler of his dynasty, he is bound to be portrayed subsequently with the characteristics of a 'loser'. This myth is clearly the 'charter' of a new dynasty, written down by its official historians. Other brief explanations occur so frequently in Chinese histories that they become stereotyped, sometimes alliterative or rhymed, like the formulas *kuan pi min pien* (officials oppress, the people rebel) or *nei-luan wai huan* (internal disorder, external disaster). It does not take much imagination to relate the Chinese attitude to historical explanation to the other characteristics of official history in a bureaucratic society. As Professor Balazs put it, 'history was written by officials for officials'.

## 3  Towards a Sociology of Historiography[1]

The value of the study of Chinese historians within the framework of this essay is that it suggests why the Renaissance had its particular sense of the past. It is always easier to be aware of the social factors which influence thinking when they are at work in another culture.

[1] The following concluding remarks are intended to put forward highly provisional explanatory hypotheses which there is not space to justify.

To a westerner who reads about Chinese histories, it seems clear that they were written in this way because of certain characteristics of Chinese society; because it was traditionalist and bureaucratic, for example. More generally, I should like to suggest that a sense of historical perspective is impossible in a society where men forget the past; it is impossible in a society where men identify with the past; it is only possible somewhere in between.

Why should men in some societies forget the past? Because, as the anthropological study of primitive societies has shown (above, p. 19), oral tradition tends to remake the past in the shape of the present. It looks as if literacy is necessary to the sense of historical perspective. Why should men in some societies identify with the past? It seems plausible to suggest that this is because the pace of social change is slow there, so that men do not experience their difference from the past for themselves. This explanatory model, if it is correct, would account for the fact that three periods with a sense of historical perspective are late antiquity, the Renaissance, and, above all, Europe after the French and Industrial Revolutions. China, which had literacy without rapid social change, and Greece, which in the age of Thucydides had social change without widespread literacy, both lacked this perspective. It is interesting to find that the Renaissance, the age when men began to think of the past as different from the present, was also the age of the discovery of a wider world – of awareness that elsewhere is different; and the age of utopian literature – of awareness that the future can be different. Perhaps these three extensions of the imagination are connected. Galileo praised change in the physical universe at a time, the early seventeenth century, when historians were becoming more aware of change in the world of man.

Again, the rise of historical scepticism, the criticism of documents and myths, may well be related to other trends in European history between the fifteenth and the seventeenth centuries. Historical scepticism is related to philosophical scepticism, on the rise between Erasmus and Descartes. Behind both movements of scepticism lay the Reformation, a successful attack on tradition which led to a situation where Catholics and Protestants each worked to undermine the foundations of the other. Protestants were sceptical of the authority of the Pope; Catholics, of the authority of the Bible. Behind the Reformation lay the great 'information explosion' of the sixteenth century, the cause of which was technological; the invention and spread of printing. Printing also made a direct impact on the writing of history. The conditions of historical labour were dramatically transformed when editions of sources could be produced and large libraries formed. An author ceased to be treated as an 'authority' when he could be easily compared with many others.

Lastly, the increasing interest in historical explanation at the Renaissance can itself be explained. Medieval chronicles tended to be of two sorts; those written by clergy for clergy, and those written by nobles for nobles. Both lacked an interest in explanation, for opposite reasons. The clerical historian had a view of history too long-term for explanation as I defined it. In a perspective which stretched from the Creation to the Last Judgement, any precise accounting for particular events must have seemed a triviality, an irrelevance. The aristocratic historian's view of history was, on the contrary, too short-term for explanation; he was interested in the noble feats of arms performed by knights. It was the details of the fighting that mattered, not the reasons for the war in which the fighting occurred. The Renaissance interest in a middle level of explanation may well be linked to a change in the authorship and readership of histories. Instead of clerics and knights, humanists and politicians now wrote history, and wrote it for the educated but civilian layman. Their interests were man-centered rather than God-centered, but concerned with strategy (political as well as military), rather than with blow-by-blow accounts of single combats. Behind these changes in authorship and readership lay general changes in social and political structures; the rise of humanists, city-states, new monarchies. In other words, the history of the writing of history is itself part of history. The Renaissance sense of the past was shaped by the awareness, and by the fact, of social change.

# FOR FURTHER READING

A short list, limited to books and articles in English.

## 1 Renaissance historical thought

F. Gilbert, *Machiavelli and Guicciardini*, Princeton, 1965.

M. P. Gilmore, *Humanists and Jurists*, Cambridge, Mass., 1963, (especially 'The Renaissance Conception of the Lessons of History' and 'Individualism in Renaissance Historians').

D. R. Kelley, 'Guillaume Budé and the First Historical School of Law' in *American Historical Review*, 72, 1966-7.

T. D. Kendrick, *British Antiquity*, London, 1950.

F. J. Levy, *Tudor Historical Thought*, San Marino, 1967.

J. G. Mann, 'Instances of Antiquarian Feeling in Medieval and Renaissance Art', in *Archaeological Journal*, 89, 1932.

J. Pocock, *The Ancient Constitution and the Feudal Law*, Cambridge, 1957.

F. Saxl, 'Jacopo Bellini and Mantegna as Antiquarians' in his *Lectures*, London, 1957.

R. H. Tawney, 'Harrington's Interpretation of his Age' in *Proceedings of the British Academy* 27, 1941.

R. Weiss, 'Petrarch the Antiquarian' in *Studies in Honour of B. L. Ullman*, Rome, 1964.

R. Weiss, *The Renaissance Discovery of Classical Antiquity*, Oxford, Blackwell, 1969.

## 2 Other Periods

E. Balazs, 'History as a Guide to Bureaucratic Practice' in his *Chinese Civilisation and Bureaucracy*, New Haven, 1964.

M. Bloch, *Feudal Society*, English trans., London, 1961 (ch. vi, viii).

H. Butterfield, *Man on His Past*, Cambridge, 1955.

R. C. Dentan, ed., *The Idea of History in the Ancient Near East*, New Haven, 1955.

E. Eisenstein, A. Momigliano and others, *History and Theory*, Beiheft 6, 1966.

M. Finley, 'Myth, Memory and History' in *History and Theory*, 4, 1965.

C. W. Jones, *Saints' Lives and Chronicles in Early England*, Ithaca, 1947.

A. Momigliano, *Studies in Historiography*, New York, 1966.

E. Neff, *The Poetry of History*, New York, 1947 (on the 19th century).

J. Pocock, 'The Origins of the Study of the Past' in *Comparative Studies in Society and History*, 5, 1962-3.

E. G. Pulleyblank, 'Chinese Historical Criticism' in Beasley and Pulleyblank, eds., *Historians of China and Japan*, Oxford, 1961.

T. R. Tholfsen, *Historical Thinking*, New York, 1967.

H. R. Trevor-Roper, 'The Historical Philosophy of the Enlightenment' in T. Besterman, ed., *Studies on Voltaire and the 18th century*, XXIV/XXVII, Oxford, 1962.

I. Watt and J. Goody, 'The Consequences of Literacy' in *Comparative Studies* in *Society and History*, 5 1962–3, reprinted in J. Goody, ed., *Literacy in Traditional Society*, Cambridge, 1968.

G. Williams, *Tradition and Originality in Roman Poetry*, Oxford, 1968 (excursus, 'The Roman View of Historical Explanation').

## CHRONOLOGICAL TABLE

1350 Petrarch's letter to Livy

1355 Petrarch, *On the falsity of the Privilege*

1415 Bruni, *History of the Florentine people*

1439 Valla, *Donation of Constantine*

1446 Biondo, *Rome Restored*

1449 Valla, *Annotations on the New Testament*

1459 Biondo, *Rome Triumphant*

1496 Colet, *Lectures on St. Paul to the Corinthians*

1499 P. Vergil, *On Inventors*

1514 Budé, *On the as*

1516 Erasmus, *Life of Jerome*

1532 Machiavelli, *Florentine Histories* (posthumous publication)

1550 Vasari, *Lives*

1555 Vico, *Discourses on Ancient Medals*

1560 Patrizzi, *Ten dialogues on History*

1560 Pasquier, *Researches about France* (Book I)

1561–7 Guicciardini, *History of Italy* (posthumous publication)

1566 Bodin, *Method*

1566 Cujas, ed., *The Book of Fiefs*

1567 Hotman, *Anti-Tribonian*

1586 Camden, *Britannia*

1614 Casaubon, *On Sacred Matters*

1614 Selden, *Titles of Honour*

1618 Selden, *History of Tithes*

1619 Sarpi, *History of the Council of Trent*

1623 Bacon, *De Augmentis* (Latin version of Advancement of Learning)

1630 Davila, *Civil Wars in France*

1639 Spelman, *On Feuds* (finished)

1643 Bollandists began The lives of the Saints

1644 Clarendon began his History

1650 Ussher, *Annals of the Old and New Testament*

1656 Harrington, *Oceana*

1666 Daillé, *On the writings known as those of Dionysius*

1670 Spinoza, *Theological-Political Treatise*